MISTAKEN

IDENTITY

Arab Stereotypes in Popular Writing

by Janice J. Terry

D1051745

American-Arab Affairs Council
1730 M Street, N.W., Suite 512, Washington, D.C. 20036
Telephone: (202) 296-6767 • Intl. Telex: 440506 AMARA

Published by the
American-Arab Affairs Council
1730 M Street, N.W., Suite 512
Washington, D.C. 20036
Tel: (202) 296-6767
Telex: 440506 AMARA UI

Library of Congress Catalog Card Number: 85-72494

ISBN 0-943182-02-6

Table of Contents

ACKNOWLEDGMENTS

I was six years old when I learned about stereotypes. Somewhere, somehow, I heard that Jewish people had big noses. Well, my father—handsome though he is—has a markedly large proboscis. So I immediately asked, "Are you Jewish?" He shrugged and said, "No."

Clearly, I had to look elsewhere. The next best place seemed to be church, where I would certainly see lots of people. The next Sunday I took careful note of everyone as they filed into the sanctuary. What luck! A family directly across from mine all had noses at least as large as my father's.

On the way home I rather gleefully announced that the family across from us in church was Jewish.

Father laughed so hard it was sometime before he answered that I was talking about the Faris family. They were from Lebanon and they were Presbyterians. He then asked why I was so interested in knowing who was Jewish.

I replied that I had heard Jewish people had large noses.

Father then said that so-and-so and so-and-so were Jewish. I knew these people very well, but every one of them had a rather small nose.

What my father said next became a life-long lesson.

"Janice, no group of people all look alike, talk alike or think alike. Generalities about others are usually based on ignorance—be careful not to fall into the trap of believing them."

Since that time I have had many more encounters with stereotypes. Sadly, they are nowhere more apparent than in the general public's attitudes about the Middle East.

Many friends and colleagues have willingly provided suggestions and assistance in this exploration of stereotypes in popular literature. Drs. Nabih Faris, Abdul Wahab Kayyali and Joseph Malone were all in their own special ways important contributors to my education and enlightenment about the Middle East and its peoples. I am indebted to Sameer Abraham for his readiness to debate interpretations and definitions. The critical interest of Michael Sulieman and, from the Arab-American Media Society, Warren David, Michael Daher and Nabeel Abraham, was equally helpful. Tom Shaw has done a marvelous job in checking and rechecking sources and bibliographic materials.

A special note of thanks goes to James Monnig's Bookstore in Detroit for providing an endless supply of paperbacks. I am also grateful to Anne Joyce for her meticulous editing of the manuscript. My husband, Donald Burke, has been constant in his support—more important, he has cheerfully lived amid ever-growing piles of newspapers, clippings and paperback books. Each of these individuals has made a unique contribution to the completion of the project.

Stereotypes—both pejorative and positive—are virtually universal. Because negative stereotypes and erroneous historical interpretations regarding the Middle East have been so persistently reinforced in every medium, large numbers of people, particularly in the Western world, continue to base their images of Arabs and the Islamic world solely on these fallacious representations. In some measure this study is an exercise in consciousness raising, for it seeks to expose and dispel the biased images of the Middle East that have been perpetrated in popular literature. The study will have been well worth the effort if upon its completion readers are left with an increased awareness of the complexities and historical realities of the Arab world.

I. INTRODUCTION

Western writers have long had a love-hate relationship with the Middle East. The Arab-Israeli conflict, the recent economic growth of the region and its strategic importance have replaced exoticism as a source of fascination for writers of novels, histories and biographies. Books on the Middle East which are aimed at a mass audience command attention not only as reading matter, but also for their influence in forming and reinforcing attitudes held by the Western public. This study is an analysis of the representations of the Middle East and its peoples as set forth in a wide variety of popular writing.

Popular writing, in paperback and hardcover forms, is aimed at the widest possible audience. It differs both quantitatively and qualitatively from publications geared to specialists, academics or the relatively few readers of critically acclaimed, but commercially less successful fiction. These publications include novels, biographies, autobiographies, first-hand accounts of current events and lavish photographic productions. Often called coffee-table display pieces, the latter focus on spectacular full-page color prints or photographs with short journalistic commentaries. Because they generally have a paucity of narrative, they are not included in this overview; however, their themes and subject matter tend to duplicate those of popular writing.

Popular publications are sold everywhere—in bookstores, airports, drugstores, and corner markets. To attract the buyer's attention, these books are often jacketed in eye-catching covers. Advertisements in red print and boldface lettering tout the books as "blood freezing," "truly frightening," or the "true inside story of an exploit that makes any fiction look tame." Bookstore displays often feature the latest arrivals. These books are extensively publicized in trade journals and book review sections in daily newspapers. As a result, the attention of the reading public is aroused and best-sellers are born which affect public opinion far more than works that might have more literary or scholarly merit, but that are more academic in tone, less dramatic in appeal and that receive less publicity and distribution.

Best-sellers also attract attention in other media. A best-seller or a book written by a well-known author is more likely to be reviewed, not only in leading publications such as *The New York Times* Sunday book review section or the *New York Review of Books*, but in magazines and newspapers throughout the United States and Europe. The average big-city daily may receive notices of over 300 books a week. Of these, only four to eight might be reviewed in the large Sunday edition and another eight to ten noted during the week, for an average of approximately 64 reviews each month.[1] Selections of books to be reviewed are based on practical considerations and the personal preferences of the reviewers. The works of noted authors such as Philip Roth, Saul Bellow and Joan Didion are always reviewed, as are books by authors with a track record for generating best-sellers, such as James Michener, or by well-known political or international personalities.

Publicity tours and interviews with authors, almost always arranged by the publishers, also markedly increase the likelihood of coverage, not only in newspapers, but on radio and television as well. Books that have enjoyed huge sales and wide public attention are also likely to be excerpted or serialized in popular magazines such as *Reader's Digest* or *People*. In addition, best-sellers form the bulk of the selections of Book-of-the-Month and other book clubs.

Clearly, more and more books are available for an ever-expanding audience. In spite of video games and a myriad of leisure-time activities, people are reading more. The number of books published in the United States alone has increased from 11,000 annually in 1950 to 50,000 in 1983.[2] At the same time, library circulations

---

[1] Information from Barbara Holliday, *The Detroit Free Press* Book Editor, 1983. In addition, specialty books, for example those on sports, might be covered in the appropriate sections of the newspaper.

[2] *The New York Times*, September 8, 1983.

have also burgeoned. Many popular English-language publications, particularly best-sellers, are translated into other languages and subsequently become best-sellers in Italy, Germany or elsewhere.[3] As financial exigencies have forced university and specialty presses to decrease their publication lists, books aimed for the mass market clearly constitute a large portion of the books in print. A great many of these popular publications, particularly in the field of fiction, deal with the Middle East, the Arab-Israeli conflict and the Arab world, all of which have a proven record of popularity.

The consolidation of publishing companies and the growing tendency toward corporate ownership of print and broadcasting firms have resulted in books with high sales receiving even more media attention. Many of the popular books dealing with the Arab-Israeli conflict or other Middle Eastern themes are published by firms that control book clubs or larger communications organizations.

In keeping with attempts to lower publishing costs and to increase profit margins, publishers often issue books in hardcover and paperback simultaneously in Great Britain and the United States. Joint publications enable publishers to lower costs while ensuring maximum distribution, sales and publicity. For example, Bantam publishes a number of "instant" histories on Israel, including those by William Stevenson. Although Doubleday had the hardcover rights to *Exodus*, Bantam acquired the profitable paperback rights. Bantam's list also includes a number of popular histories of World War II. In Great Britain Corgi Press, which is owned by Transworld Publishers, has published a number of books on the Middle East. Another British firm, Collins, acted as publisher for both the late Egyptian President Anwar Sadat and Mohamed Heikal, the former editor of the renowned Egyptian newspaper, *Al-Ahram*. Rights to Sadat's autobiography were acquired by Harper and Row in the United States; the autobiography was also excerpted in *Time* magazine.

---

[3]*The New York Times*, October 18, 1983.

A number of popular books dealing with the Middle East are published by Popular Library, Fawcett, and Holt, Rinehart and Winston, all of which are controlled by CBS, which owns several other publishing firms. The CBS conglomerate ownership of such a wide range of publishing houses, plus its control of one of the major U.S. broadcasting firms, has been investigated by the antitrust division of the U.S. Department of Justice. On August 19, 1979, *The New York Times* noted that the antitrust division was interested "not in business per se, but rather in access by authors, publishers, and potential new houses to the marketplace, and in what that possible lack of access portends for consumers—in this case readers."[4]

Similarly, another publishing giant, Doubleday, is divided into divisions and subsidiaries including several dozen bookstores, Dial Press, Dell, Literary Guild and a lucrative broadcasting subsidiary. Indeed Doubleday's corporate ownership is so wide and varied that it has called itself a "communications company."[5] Times Inc., with ownership of Book-of-the-Month Club, Filmways, Grosset and Dunlap, and Warner Communications with Warner Books are other huge publishing and communications conglomerates. Likewise, large book store chains increasingly dominate sales. Dalton and Waldenbooks run more than 1500 bookstores across the nation. As these chains continue to expand, smaller independent stores find it harder to survive. Because these giants generally control the bulk of the popular book market, major changes in the types or style of popular writing are unlikely. As the financial considerations of publishing have become increasingly important, decision-makers tend to rely on those types of publications that have proven records of profitability.

Commercially successful books also attract movie, television and theatrical producers. The film and television rights to best-

---

[4]Herbert Mitgang, "Mergers in the Book World; Still an Unfinished Chapter," *The New York Times*, Sunday, August 19, 1979.

[5]Edward Tivnan, "Doubleday Rocks and Rolls," *New York* magazine, February 7, 1983.

selling novels are often sold for astronomical amounts. The dramatic adaptations of these best-sellers are widely advertised and publicized through interviews, reviews and public appearances of those involved with the production. When a best-selling book receives total media coverage, the content of the book, in a variety of forms, reaches virtually all segments of the Western public— even those that do not actually read popular books. Consequently, best-sellers based on themes, events or characters from the Middle East can, and often do, influence far greater numbers than the initial readers.

The peoples, religions, history and conflicts of the Middle East are described in remarkably similar terms in most popular books. With the exception of the novel *Exodus*, which is in many ways a prototype for contemporary novels dealing with the Middle East, the books under discussion have all been published in the last twenty years. *Exodus* has been followed by a number of novels based on the historical conflicts in Palestine. Novels like *The Source* by James Michener and *Promise the Earth* by Clive Irving are highly reminiscent of *Exodus*, both in form and in the authors' pro-Israeli sympathies. Like most Michener novels, *The Source* was an enormous commercial success. Norman Mailer's peculiar erotic representation of Pharaonic Egypt, *Ancient Evenings*, is another recent historical novel based on a highly romanticized version of the Middle East. Although not a critical success, the novel received the publicity and fanfare that accompanies anything written by Mailer.

The majority of the books under consideration in this study have been published in the last ten years; most are readily available to buyers and readers. Although only a small sample of the large number of books dealing with Middle Eastern themes is discussed, a representative cross-section has been selected. For purposes of analysis, the material has been divided into separate categories: biographies and autobiographies, popular or "instant" histories, romances, adventure stories, novels of financial intrigue, mysteries and tales of espionage exploits.

This study is not an exercise in literary criticism. Nor does it attempt to weigh the long-term literary value (if any) of the works. The books under discussion vary tremendously in their relative literary merits. They have not been selected for discussion because of style but because each provides some insight into how the Middle East is treated in contemporary writing.

Autobiographies and biographies of well-known Middle Eastern leaders have been selected on the basis of their sales and impacts. Several of these have been adapted into plays, films or docu-dramas made for television. The renowned authors bring a unique personal perspective to their descriptions of the region. Popular histories tend to focus on the various Arab-Israeli wars or on specific highly publicized and sensationalized events. Because a discussion of all the "instant" histories based on the 1967 or 1973 Arab-Israeli wars would be both protracted and repetitious, a few representative works have been selected. Again, books by well-known authors have been chosen over those which might be more factual but less popular with the general audience.

The sheer quantity of novels based on the Middle East made choosing typical examples extremely difficult. There was also the problem of never-ending supply. It was a major task just keeping track of the most recent titles. Here again, books by critically acclaimed and/or highly popular writers were preferred choices. A few examples were selected on the basis of an eye-catching cover or title, much as the average browser would purchase a book for recreational reading. In a few instances a novel was chosen, not for its individual impact, but because it was representative of an entire genre in which one example is very much like countless others. Some are featured because they offer an offbeat or unusual interpretation. Enthusiasts of popular fiction may find their particular favorite or most despised novel about the Middle East missing from the discussion. Practically speaking, alluding to all the possible examples in one study of manageable length is not only virtually impossible but pointless as well. For the purposes of clarity and classification, popular fiction has been divided into major genres—romances, adventures, mysteries—from which a representative sampling has then been described and analyzed.

Historical Perspective

Before turning to specific examples, it is necessary to provide a short historical perspective and to clarify some terms. Western attitudes regarding the Middle East have been formed over many centuries. Recently the media—films, television, radio, newspapers, magazines, textbooks, and popular writing—have deluged the Western public with images of the Arab and Muslim worlds, Israel and the Middle East in general. Media representations, together with religious and historical interpretations, many of which date back to the Middle Ages, form the basis for most Western concepts of the Middle East.

In this regard, Edward Said's arguments posited in his provocative *Orientalism* and *Covering Islam* have special validity.[6] In *Orientalism*, by far the denser and more erudite of the two works, Said argues that the West has long held a complex body of prejudicial stereotypes about Muslims and Arabs, who are seen as interchangeable and not as distinct entities. The nature of the contact between the West and the Arab and much of the Islamic world has frequently been confrontational. In France, Spain, the Balkans, Eastern Europe and the eastern Mediterranean during the Crusades, Western and Middle Eastern empires clashed on the field of battle. Religious and cultural differences further exacerbated the conflict. Consequently, Western literature, folklore and academic writing have long reflected largely negative attitudes toward the Middle East. In recent years the Arab-Israeli conflict coupled with strategic and economic concerns have aggravated these long-held enmities. Television news has brought current political events in the Middle East unrelentingly into the lives of the Western public. Because oversimplifications are inherent in the brief news capsules used to convey information in that medium,

---

[6]Edward Said, *Orientalism*, New York: Pantheon Books, 1978; *Covering Islam*, New York: Pantheon Books, 1981.

stereotyping is the rule rather than the exception. There is no time or inclination to add complexity by individualizing the newsmakers. Stereotypes used in one medium feed into others, both reflecting and perpetuating old prejudices and distortions.

For the purposes of this study, *stereotype* may be defined as a "mental package" in which a collection of traits or characteristics are combined to delineate or identify a group or a member of that group without reference to particular individual differences or complexities. More often than not, these "identifying characteristics" are half-truths which distort or obfuscate the full reality. On both conscious and subconscious levels people may accept stereotypes as factual representations.

Because stereotypes are so common and because they frequently have been assimilated on the subconscious level, they are hard to dispel. Edmund Ghareeb in *Split Vision: The Portrayal of Arabs in the American Media*, has emphasized that stereotypes often "provide a convenient shorthand in the identification of a particular group."[7] Stereotypes form the basis for ethnic, religious or racial *prejudice*. This preconceived judgment is an emotional response rather than a cognitive one.

The foundation of prejudice is a mental representation or *image* that does not completely correspond to reality. When applied to individuals or groups it has a dehumanizing effect. Prejudice is often the basis for negative *attitudes* or positions that may be identified by feelings or actions. Hence, a causal cycle has been set in motion. Stereotypes often lead to prejudice based on erroneous or distorted images that, in turn, result in negative attitudes or actions.

Over the centuries, numerous negative stereotypes of the Middle East, in particular of Arabs and Muslims, have been endlessly

---

[7]Edmund Ghareeb, ed., *Split Vision: The Portrayal of Arabs in the American Media*, Washington, D.C., American-Arab Affairs Council, 1983. For a fuller exposition on the causes and operations of prejudice see Gordon Allport, *On the Nature of Prejudice*, Cambridge, Mass: Addison-Wesley, 1954, and Bruno Bettelheim and Morris Janowitz, *Dynamics of Prejudice*, New York: Harper and Row, 1950.

reinforced in the West. The very experts who have allegedly sought to "explain" the Middle East have contributed to perpetuating and legitimatizing these stereotypes.[8] Even respected academics have often analyzed the Middle East solely from Western and/or Christian perspectives.

Although studies that purport to examine the Italian, African or Mexican "mind" have long been discredited, works that allegedly explain the totality of Arabs and Muslims still abound. For example, John Laffin in *Rhetoric and Reality: The Arab Mind Considered* has described the Arab world in a particularly negative manner. This work was originally published in Great Britain under the title *The Arab Mind*.[9] Subsequently, Laffin wrote *The Dagger of Islam*, which is, in fact, another anti-Muslim diatribe masquerading as an objective, scholarly account of "what every thinking person should know about one of the world's most potent political forces—Islam."[10] Reasonably priced, the Bantam paperback edition was clearly aimed for the mass market and was widely distributed in national bookstore chains. In spite of the misleading advertising surrounding *The Dagger of Islam*, it in no way approaches the far more balanced and thoughtful studies, *Faith and Power: The Politics of Islam* by Edward Mortimer or *Militant Islam* by Godfrey Jansen.[11]

In contrast to Laffin, both Mortimer and Jansen seek to explain the complexities of Islam; both studies describe the role of religion

---

[8]See Sania Hamady, *Temperament and Character of the Arabs*, New York: Twayne Publishers, 1960, and Morroe Berger, *The Arab World Today*, New York: Anchor Books, 1964, for studies that attempt sweeping descriptions of the Arabs. Michael W. Suleiman in "Fact and Fiction in American Perceptions of the Middle East" (unpublished paper) and in "Stereotypes, Public Opinion and Foreign Policy," *Action*, February 7, 14, 21, 1983, has noted these distortions at much greater length; he also discusses their impact on inaccurate analyses of Arab military and diplomatic policies.

[9]John Laffin, *Rhetoric and Reality: The Arab Mind Considered*, New York: Taplinger Publishing, 1975.

[10]John Laffin, *The Dagger of Islam*, New York: revised edition, Bantam, 1981; Sphere, 1979. Back cover of paperback Bantam edition.

[11]Edward Mortimer, *Faith and Power: The Politics of Islam*, New York: Vintage, 1982; Godfrey Jansen, *Militant Islam*, New York: Harper and Row, 1979.

in the vastly different, yet still Islamic, societies of Iran, Egypt, Pakistan and parts of the Soviet Union. The Iranian revolution and the demand by many Muslims for a return to more spiritual, rather than secular societies are approached, not from hostile positions, but from what more nearly approximates Islamic perspectives.

Contemporary Approaches

Recently, the well-respected writers V.S. Naipaul in *Among the Believers* and Jonathan Raban in *Arabia through the Looking Glass*[12] have both written about their personal experiences in the Islamic nations of Iran and the Arabian peninsula. Like many first-hand travel accounts, these two books reveal more about the authors than about the societies they seek to explain. In particular, Naipaul seems unable or unwilling to extricate himself from his own personal history. His Hindu and Indian heritage and his upbringing in pre-independent Trinidad seem to color his reactions to Iran during the revolution. Naipaul has the eye for detail of a literary artist, but it is a selective eye that often reflects inward. Raban's *Arabia through the Looking Glass* is a more superficial look at the various nations in the Arabian peninsula. Yet it, too, tends to mirror Raban's reactions to what he sees rather than the three dimensional qualities of the Arab world. Of course, readers of travelers' accounts of their journeys know at the outset that, by definition, these are personal stories—indeed, that is one of their charms. Travel books are not publicized as objective or scholarly studies; readers expect a personal interpretation of writers' experiences. The popularity of contemporary travel books about the Middle East attests to the widespread interest in the region among Western readers.

Science fiction is another genre in which themes based on aspects of the Middle East are sometimes used, but readers of "sci-fi"

---

[12]V.S. Naipaul, *Among the Believers*, New York: Alfred Knopf, Inc., 1981; Vintage, 1982; Jonathan Raban, *Arabia Through the Looking Glass*, London: William Collins, 1979, Fontana, 1980.

10

recognize from the outset that the material is fantasy. The well-known *Dune* books by Frank Herbert are among the most popular science fiction novels that deal extensively with language, tribes and geographical conditions that are remarkably similar to the Arab world. Ironically, these '''"fantasies" often more closely and objectively approximate the Arab world than many novels that supposedly recreate reality. Because travel accounts and science fiction do not purport to render "true to life" or exact representations of the Middle East, they are mentioned only in passing and are not included in the more detailed analysis of popular writing based on Middle Eastern subjects.

The recent interest in the Middle East and Islam is, of course, closely associated with the political, military and economic importance of the region. The Cold War, the Arab-Israeli conflict, the anxiety about the supply of petroleum resources, and the Iranian revolution have all increased the Western appetite for news and information; this increased demand has made the Middle East an attractive subject for popular literature. The premises of plots and the characterizations of leading figures in much popular fiction are based on both old stereotypes and contemporary political considerations. Fiction is a particularly sympathetic medium for the presentation of specific political viewpoints. The political bent of a large quantity of popular writing is apparent in many books in which the Iranian revolution, Arab nationalism and the Arab-Israeli conflict play a role.

Zionist partisans have been consistently successful in using popular literary forms to present the Israeli case. As Westerners, they usually held the same distorted images of the Middle East as did their contemporaries. Zionists advanced the argument that they would bring a superior, Western culture to the area, emphasizing that Israel would be an Occidental outpost in the otherwise alien Orient. Before 1967, the Western public generally perceived Israelis as courageous underdogs struggling against the Arab enemy which sought to destroy the only democratic nation in the pro-Soviet, totalitarian Middle East. The image of the Arab-Israeli conflict in popular writing has reflected this one-sided view.

Although Zionist publicity efforts initially were aimed at converting European and American Jewish communities, the scope was gradually broadened to include the general public. Zionist supporters quickly realized the effectiveness of popular literature as a means of establishing and reinforcing sympathy for Israel. Leon Uris's *Exodus*, which will be discussed in a subsequent chapter, remains the outstanding example of the power of a best-selling novel to shape public opinion. For many, the story of Israel's creation as described in *Exodus* remains the only valid account. No matter how many times the factual case may be presented, the dramatic—albeit misleading or false—version has, in the public imagination, assumed the force of truth.

On the other side, a novelist who might wish to describe Arabs or the Arab-Israeli conflict in a more objective fashion has first to dispel the negative stereotypes of the Arab and Muslim worlds. Because negative images often have been assimilated subconsciously, many Westerners are unaware of the deeper causes for their latent hostility toward the Arabs and Muslims. For many Westerners, it appears that their support for Israel and opposition to the Arab world springs solely from a desire to see a people grievously wronged given some measure of retribution.

Then, too, Arabs have been woefully ignorant of the mechanisms under which Western media operate. They also tend to lack reputable spokespeople in the media. Having few active political constituencies in the West, the Arabs have traditionally failed to exert extensive political influence in Europe or the United States. Similarly, they have found it difficult to gain access to those in decision-making positions. Consequently, the Arab side of the Arab-Israeli conflict, as well as other issues of vital interest to nations in both the Middle East and the West, have not been widely publicized. Thus it is not at all surprising that the Arab side has rarely, if ever, been given sympathetic attention in popular writing.

Even in the current climate of opinion, which is much more favorably disposed toward the Arab world than that of the 1960s or 1970s, there are very few fictional accounts that are sympathetic to the Arabs or Muslims. The popular books aimed for the mass market are all remarkably similar. The authors employ many of the same techniques that are found in effective propaganda. However, they have the additional advantage of writing fiction, wherein the author's only limitation is the extent to which the reader is willing to suspend disbelief. As will be demonstrated, this willingness is almost boundless in the case of novels about the Middle East. Nor do novelists have to explain or justify their use of literary devices that would be unacceptable in more scholarly writing. Value judgments, generalizations, innuendo, sarcasm, stereotyping, historical omission and tag words are among the devices used in popular literature. Literary license allows writers of fiction and even of "instant" histories the advantage of presenting a particular viewpoint without the constraint of objectivity or the necessity of having to furnish complete documentation. Novels based on historical or contemporary events can, and often do, impart distorted or completely misleading interpretations. However, because these works have great dramatic power, their impact on readers surpasses that of drier, more scholarly renditions.

Similarly, the authors of "instant" histories often fail to cite references. Owing to the enormous pressure to rush the book to print while the public is still interested in an ongoing crisis, the authors of popular histories frequently base their works on incomplete documentation or on extremely limited research.

In autobiographical works aimed for the general public, the authors usually make their viewpoints clear from the beginning. More often than not, memoirs and autobiographies are a convenient method for a well-known personality to clarify and justify his or her actions as they relate to public events. With backgrounds in Western culture and language, Israeli leaders have been particularly prolific in writing personal accounts for Western audiences. Not surprisingly, the autobiographies of Golda Meir, Ezer Weizman and Moshe Dayan, to name just a few, are predicated on a belief in Zionism. Although occasionally critical of specific Israeli leaders or policies, these authors wholeheartedly support Zionism and Israel.

There are relatively few popular autobiographical accounts by Arab leaders, partly due to cultural and linguistic differences. There is a similar paucity of biographies of Arab leaders, whereas there are numerous such works on Israeli leaders, almost all of which are positive in tone. Popular biographies of Arab leaders, with few exceptions, tend to present Arabs and specific Arab leaders in highly negative if not completely distorted terms. When the reader is only exposed to these slanted accounts, to the exclusion of opposing views, misleading impressions and conclusions result.

Instant or popular histories often contain the same sorts of distortions and biases. There are many popular works available that purport to present objective analyses of the Arab-Israeli conflict, but which are, in fact, vehicles for Zionist ideals. Several such works, particularly by William Stevenson, will be discussed. Novelists also tend to depict the conflict from the Israeli perspective and to ignore or to discount the long, complex historical background behind continued Arab and Israeli differences. In popular writing the Arabs are generally depicted in negative stereotypes and the Israelis tend to be characterized in positive terms. As the Arab-Israeli conflict has attracted public interest, it has also become a frequent subject for Western novelists, who tend to present the conflict as a contest between the forces for good (meaning Western) and the forces for evil (meaning Oriental or Middle Eastern). Very rarely does such material provide the reader with a three-dimensional image of the region or of the people struggling for the expression of their rights. Hence the Western public continues to be exposed to a constantly reinforced, distorted image of the dynamics of the principal conflict as well as of the Middle East as a whole. The following chapters will offer a brief overview and analysis of those images, distortions and stereotypes as they have appeared on the pages of numerous popular books in the recent past.

II. EXODUS
A Prototype of Popular Literature
on the Middle East

The prototype for contemporary fiction based on Middle Eastern themes is *Exodus* by Leon Uris. Copyrighted in 1958, it had enjoyed 55 printings in paperback form by 1978.[1] Advertised as "one of the Great Bestselling Novels of all time," *Exodus* has had a massive impact on the Western audience. "Exodus," the hugely successful film starring Paul Newman, reinforced and broadened the novel's influence. Later United Artists sold it to over one-hundred television stations across the country, each of which shows the film on the average of twice a year. Despite its advanced age, it continues to reach a massive audience.

Media personnel are themselves well aware of the deleterious impact television dramas and films can have on audiences, particularly young people. The syndicated columnist Nick Thimmesch, among others, has pointed out that the majority of film admissions are purchased by people under thirty-five. Thimmesch has also emphasized that it takes "many high-quality news programs to undo the damage caused by a single stereotype-laden prime-time drama."[2] He goes on to note that the same considerations apply to films. Through the book, film and television re-runs, *Exodus* has reached several generations of Americans. With little knowledge of the Middle East, the average Western reader or viewer all too often confuses fictionalized accounts such as *Exodus* with historical reality.

---

[1]Leon Uris, *Exodus*, New York: Bantam, 1978.
[2]Nick Thimmesch, "American Media Perspectives on the Arab World," in *The American Media and the Arabs*, ed. by Michael C. Hudson and Ronald G. Wolfe, Washington: Center for Contemporary Arab Studies, Georgetown University, 1980, pp. 60-61.

Briefly, the plot of *Exodus* revolves around the involvement of an American nurse with the struggle to create the new state of Israel. Set against a backdrop of armed struggle and hardship, the novel is peopled with the predictable hard-nosed journalist, the tormented British officer, the beautiful young Jewess, and the toughened young Israeli men who are always referred to as freedom fighters.

For millions of readers the novel *Exodus* stands as the definitive account of Israel's creation. The events and people described seem real, particularly as embodied by the glamorous Hollywood stars in the film. The images of the Middle East have become the reader's conception of the reality. How often one hears the remark, "but in *Exodus* it said . . ." followed by a recitation of how events happened in the novel. Uris purposely exacerbates the confusion by claiming in his dedication that "most of the events in *Exodus* are a matter of history and public record." Uris reiterates this claim in *The Haj* , his latest and extremely anti-Arab novel. In truth, the history depicted in *Exodus* and *The Haj* is highly distorted and slanted.

In a direct misrepresentation of the agricultural village society that existed in Palestine, Uris continually describes the land as full of "festering stagnating swamps and eroded hills."[3] Making frequent use of hyperbole, he claims that there had been no changes in the villages for 1,000 years and that there were only "rock-filled fields and unfertile earth . . . a land denuded of its richness. It was a land that lay bleeding and fallow" (pp. 213, 216).

Uris continually returns to the theme of a "fruitless, listless, dying land" (p. 216). These descriptions reinforce the average Western concept of the entire Middle East as one vast desert. The images totally belie the reality of Palestine as an ancient agricultural region. In the early twentieth century, Palestine was still predominantly agricultural with a largely peasant society. Citrus fruits, grains and olives were the major crops. In certain parts of Palestine the hilly, rocky terrain and sporadic rainfall made it

---

[3]Uris, *op. cit.*, p. 216.

difficult to compare agricultural productivity to the more fertile parts of Europe; however, documentation clearly reveals that agriculture was well and firmly established under the Palestinian Arab peasantry. Indeed, most Jewish colonists coming into the region settled, not in the countryside, but in urban areas.[4] That Palestine was a worthless piece of real estate that only blossomed under Israeli care became one of the major Zionist myths commonly accepted by Western society. In *Exodus* Uris is responsible for the reinforcement and exaggeration of this myth, which has been used with impunity by innumerable Western writers.

Uris also badly distorts the exact nature of British actions regarding the Middle East during and after World War I. In spite of escalating interest in the Middle East, the average Westerner, particularly the American, remains largely uninformed or misinformed as to the society, culture and history of the region. In order to assess the impact of the portrayal of the Middle East in popular literature, it is necessary at this juncture to provide a brief historical overview.

Until World War I, most of the Arab world had been part of the Ottoman Empire, which had controlled the region since the sixteenth century. World War I accelerated nationalist movements throughout the region. In order to protect their imperial interests and the Suez Canal from the Ottomans, who were allied with the Central Powers in the war, the British were generally willing to assist Arab nationalists.[5] The British did not necessarily share

---

[4]John Ruedy, "Dynamics of Land Alienation," in *The Transformation of Palestine*, ed. Ibrahim Abu-Lughod, Evanston, Illinois: Northwestern University Press, 1971; see also the article, "The Demographic Transformation of Palestine" by Janet L. Abu-Lughod in the same anthology. Doreen Warriner, "Land-Tenure Problems in the Fertile Crescent in the Nineteenth and Twentieth Centuries," *The Economic History of the Middle East, 1800-1914: A Book of Readings*, ed. Charles Issawi, Chicago, University of Chicago Press, 1966, and Walter Lehn, "The Jewish National Fund," *Journal of Palestine Studies*, vol. III. no. 4, Summer 1974, also discuss land ownership and demographic issues.

[5]For a more comprehensive review of the Middle East within the context of global twentieth century history, see Richard Goff, Walter Moss, Janice Terry and Jiu-Hwa Upshur, *The Twentieth Century: a Brief Global History*, New York: A. Knopf, 1983.

17

Arab goals, but they wanted to foment an Arab revolt against the Ottoman Turks. To implement their wartime and post-war aims, the British made three agreements that thereby helped to sow the seeds for a struggle—the Arab-Israeli conflict—that has yet to be resolved.

The first agreement was in secret correspondence, 1915-16, between Henry McMahon, the British High Commissioner in Egypt, and Sherif Husayn, the leader of the Holy City of Mecca. After protracted negotiations it was agreed that the Arabs would revolt against the Ottomans in return for an independent Arab nation after the war. Owing to the imperial interests of the British and the French, Iraq and Lebanon were excluded from the agreement. However, the British made a second secret treaty, the Sykes-Picot agreement, in 1916 with the French. Under this agreement the British and the French decided to divide up the Middle East, France gaining control of Lebanon and Syria and Great Britain obtaining sovereignty over Iraq and Palestine and a sphere of influence over Saudi Arabia.

The third British statement regarding the Middle East was the Balfour Declaration of 1917, in which the British publicly stated that they "viewed with favor" the establishment of a national home in Palestine for the Jewish people. Although the statement did not say that Great Britain would support an independent Jewish state in Palestine, many Jews and non-Jews believed that such a state would be established. The Balfour Declaration was hailed as a victory by the Zionists or Jewish nationalists. However, Arab leaders condemned the Declaration and opposed the creation of a Jewish state in Palestine, where the population was almost 90 percent Arab. Many Westerners failed to recognize that by supporting Jewish nationhood, another group, the Palestinian Arabs, would lose their homeland.

After the War, the British and French were largely able to implement the secret Sykes-Picot agreement of 1916. Consequently, Great Britain received the Mandates or control over Palestine and Iraq, while the French occupied Lebanon and Syria. However, in *Exodus* the Balfour Declaration of 1917, whereby the

British appeared to support the idea of a Jewish homeland in Palestine, is depicted as the sole legitimate British agreement involving the Middle East. Because no dates are provided, the narrative in *Exodus* leaves the unwary reader with the clear-cut impression that the Sykes-Picot treaty was a later betrayal by the British. Actually, the secret Sykes-Picot agreement, wherein the British and the French agreed to divide the Ottoman territories in the Middle East, was signed in 1916—over a year before the public Balfour Declaration. The narrative does not even mention the concomitant secret correspondence in 1916 between Sherif Husayn and McMahon, wherein the British agreed to support an independent Arab state, inclusive of Palestine, after the war in exchange for Arab support during the war.

Uris also denegrates the entire Arab national movement by dismissing Faysal, Sherif Husayn's son and later King of Iraq, as the leader of "the alleged Arab revolt" (p. 252). Relying on the general public's ignorance of Middle East history, even that of the contemporary era, Uris (without fear of criticism) misrepresents, dismisses and distorts well-documented historical facts.

The period of the British Mandate over Palestine is also described in highly misleading terms. In *Exodus* the British are depicted as being totally pro-Arab and as keeping their Arab puppets happy with automobiles and well-stocked harems (pp. 31, 252). Any study of the Mandate indicates that the British in Palestine were engaged in a tripartite struggle to balance Zionist and Palestinian Arab national demands in order to maintain their own control. The interwar years of the 1920s and 1930s were marked by continuous armed conflict between the Zionists and the Palestinian Arabs. The Zionists worked to translate their goals into reality through Jewish immigration and colonization and by gaining Western support. The Palestinians opposed both Zionist and British activities. In the rest of the Arab world, the British were consistently opposed by Arab nationalists. The British used a variety of military, diplomatic and economic means to remain the dominant imperial power, but providing cars and harems were not among them.

19

Uris also distorts events surrounding the decision to partition Palestine and the involvement of the United Nations to the benefit of the Israelis and to the detriment of the Palestinians and Arabs. Arabs are depicted as using "threats, boycotts, blackmail and any other pressure" (p. 369) to stop the partition of Palestine by the United Nations. No mention is made of the extensive Zionist lobby or of pressure by the United States on nations like Liberia to support partition. A more comprehensive and objective description of the Zionist political maneuverings at the United Nations is to be found in Fred J. Khouri's *The Arab-Israeli Dilemma.*[6] In a passage from *Exodus* that combines the wasteland myth with historic misrepresentation, the issue of the inclusion of the Negev into the proposed Jewish sector is described in the following terms:

> *The Arabs had millions of square miles of undeveloped waste-lands. The Jews wanted this small piece of a few thousand square miles in the hope they could redeem it* (p. 448).

The 1948 Arab-Israeli war is referred to as the "War of Liberation"; the massive exodus of Palestinian Arabs from the territory is scarcely mentioned. Nor do any of the Israeli characters admit responsibility for the refugees, who are defined as solely an Arab problem. This theme will be echoed throughout subsequent contemporary literature and reflects the general attitude of Israeli leaders such as David Ben-Gurion and Golda Meir.

Actually, the decision of the United Nations to partition Palestine and the causes of the first Arab-Israeli war in 1948 are considerably more complex than the Uris narrative implies. After 1945, both the Zionists and the Palestinian Arabs had pressed for the creation of their own individual nations in Palestine.[7] The British, who had formerly played Palestinian and Zionist nationalist movements against one another, were caught on the horns of a dilemma. Ultimately, the British admitted defeat and turned the

---

[6]Fred J. Khouri, *The Arab-Israeli Dilemma*, 2nd. ed., New York: Syracuse University Press, 1976.

[7]For an extensive description of this era see: Khouri; Abu-Lughod; and Goff, Moss, Terry and Upshur *op. cit.*

problem over to the United Nations. Under the subsequent U.N. partition plan about 50 percent of the territory, including the more fertile coastal areas, was given to the Zionists, who were about one-third of the population. Although the Zionists somewhat reluctantly accepted the plan, the Palestinian Arabs were totally opposed to it. When the British hastily withdrew on May 14, 1948, David Ben-Gurion, who had already received assurances of support from President Truman, announced the creation of the state of Israel. The surrounding Arab states and the Palestinian Arabs refused to recognize the state, and the first Arab-Israeli war promptly began.

The Israelis won the 1948 war and expanded their territory by approximately one-third more than was granted under the U.N. partition plan. Before and during the war, thousands of Palestinians, particularly the peasants, had fled their farms and homes. The Arabs maintained that the refugees had left because of Zionist terrorism. The Israelis argued that they were not responsible. Although there are cases supporting both sides, the 1948 war left almost a million Palestinians homeless. By 1979 there were over a million and a half Palestinian refugees who wanted to return to their homeland. It was from the poverty and discontent of the refugee camps that the guerrillas of the Palestinian liberation organizations who were active after 1967 were to come.

Individual Arab leaders are criticized by Uris in the most scathing terms. Mufti Husseini, who was actually opposed by many Arabs, is described as "the leader of the dreaded El Husseinis . . . the most vile, underhanded schemer in a part of the world known for vile, underhanded schemers" (p. 253). Al-Quwuqji, a noted Palestinian military commander, and his followers are labeled as "vicious, degenerate, and brutal a gang as had ever been assembled" (p. 275). Palestinian Arab fighters against the partition of 1948 are condemned as having been recruited from "the sinkholes of Damascus, Beirut and Baghdad" and defamed as being the "dregs of humanity, thieves, murderers, highway robbers, dope runners and white slavers" (p. 467). The narrative gives no indication that the Palestinian Arabs had any legitimate national rights.

21

Nor does Uris note that Fauzi al-Qawuqji's liberation army never exceeded three to four thousand fighters, of which over one-quarter were local Palestinian Arabs.[8]

The plot of *Exodus* also distorts history by its notable and misleading omissions of relevant facts and details. Place names on the several maps included in the text are always given as the Jewish names, never the Arab ones. Jewish settlers in Palestine are described as Palestinian Jews; the term Palestinian is never used in reference to Arabs. Arabs are viewed as a group rather than as individuals. In such a fashion the Palestinian Arabs lost their identity, not only in popular literature, but in the collective opinion of the Western world. For the West, Palestinian Arabs literally ceased to exist until they forced themselves upon world consciousness after 1967. This denial of Palestinian Arab existence is reflected in the public statements of Israeli leaders. Novels such as *Exodus* and many others, some of which will be discussed in subsequent chapters, have done much to foster that attitude.

Uris quite properly eschews the Jewish stereotypes present in so much Western literature. In the introduction to *Exodus* he notes that "the cliché Jewish characters who have cluttered up our American fiction—the clever businessman, the brilliant doctor, the sneaky lawyer . . . all these have been left where they rightfully belong, on the cutting-room floor." Somewhat ironically, the Jewish Israeli characters that Uris created in *Exodus* have become new—albeit positive—stereotypes: courageous, indomitable fighters who struggle only for their legitimate rights.

The concluding chapters of the novel are a paean to the new Israeli state. In the novel, Israel is "an epic history of man" (p. 572), and a "bridge between darkness and light" (p. 589). Israeli national policies are stated in the most positive terms. In contrast, no consideration is given to the geopolitical needs of the surrounding Arab nations. For example, the projected Israeli redistribution of the water from the Jordan River, a vital source of water for

---

[8]Fauzi al-Qawuqji, "Memoirs, 1948," *Journal of Palestine Studies*, vol. I, no. 4, Summer 1972.

several geographically contiguous nations, is described only as changing the course of the river "a few kilometers" (p. 591). The opposition by Arab nations to Israel's diversion of scarce water resources is dismissed as totally unwarranted and irrational. As early as 1950 Israel had plans to divert portions of the Jordan River; U.S. plans were also suggested. In general, these plans exacerbated the riparian dispute and increased conflicts, especially between Israel and Jordan. When no agreement could be reached, Israel went ahead with a unilateral plan of diversion in 1963. Israel was able to effect the diversion because of its superior military strength and the inability of Arab governments to counter the Israeli action.[9]

Uris movingly characterizes the Israelis as beleaguered people surrounded by "a million kill-crazy Arabs" (p. 588). He labels Egyptian President Nasser a "would-be Hitler" (p. 582), and accuses Arab *fedayeen* "gangs" of committing "atrocity after atrocity" (p. 582). This negative depiction of Nasser and Arab opposition to Israel obscures the real nature of Nasser's great popularity. In 1952, Nasser and a group of army officers overthrew the corrupt monarchy of King Faruq.[10] Nasser immediately proclaimed that the new regime would institute comprehensive land reform and put an end to feudalism, imperialism and corruption. The Aswan dam was the cornerstone of Nasser's program for Egyptian economic development. In addition to the huge economic improvements the dam would bring, it would also demonstrate Egypt's ability to be self-sufficient and independent of imperial domination. Nasser, a highly charismatic leader, moved Egypt toward a more neutral position within the global power struggle.

---

[9]For more details on the riparian dispute see: Robert W. Stookey, *America and the Arab States: An Uneasy Encounter*, New York: John Wiley and Sons, 1975 and Basheer K. Nijim, "The Jordan Basin and International Riparian Disputes: A Search for Patterns," Paper delivered at the Middle East Studies Association Conference, Columbus, OH, November, 1970.

[10]Peter Mansfield in *Nasser's Egypt*, London: Penguin, 1965, offers a highly readable account of Nasser's rise to power and his impact on Egypt and the rest of the Arab world.

His growing importance in the Arab world, and indeed among Third World leaders generally, was viewed as a threat by both the United States and Israel. The positive developments in Egypt under Nasser's leadership are completely ignored in *Exodus*.

The picture painted in *Exodus* is one totally and unquestionably favorable to Israel. There is no point in the narrative at which an Israeli action is described in anything but positive terms. There are no Israeli villains. Moreover, there is not a single Israeli character that has less than an exemplary character. In the jargon of popular writing, Uris has created a nation of "good-guys." This positive stereotype in *Exodus* became the model for subsequent novels dealing with the Middle East. The image has been so continuously reinforced in popular culture that it permeates the consciousness of Western society. As will be demonstrated, the favorable Western-held stereotype of Israelis had immediate positive ramifications for the nation of Israel.

Although Uris assiduously avoided the negative stereotypes— as he termed them, clichés—of Jewish characters, he did not exercise the same sensitivity regarding Arabs. Indeed, the entire novel is replete with highly negative, anti-Arab stereotypes. Uris draws from the same grab bag of literary techniques so favored by the effective propagandist. He applies value judgments, generalizations, negative labeling, omission, tag words, sarcasm and innuendo regarding his two-dimensional Arab characters and the Arab world in general. Taking full advantage of literary license, Uris dramatically presents his version of the Middle East without objectivity or balance.

The portrayal of Arabs in *Exodus* is racist, sexist and culturally biased. Arabs, whether Muslim or Christian, are described as "dirty" (pp. 334, 348), "crafty " (p. 229) and "corrupt" (p. 229). Although they are not Arabs, Turks are referred to collectively with Arabs as thieves (p. 218). Negative Arab, Iranian and Turkish stereotypes are used interchangeably in much popular writing. Attempts to differentiate among these three different ethnic groups are rarely made. The typical racist technique of generalizing from one individual to the entire group is commonly applied in *Exodus*.

At one point a "fat Arab" (p. 376) merchant insists on bargaining to make a sale. While there are individuals with a wide variety of physiques in all societies, the thrust of this passage is to stress the gross aspects of this fictional Arab merchant. The emphasis on his obesity is particularly ironic in light of specific Koranic injunctions against gluttony and excess. However, most Western readers of *Exodus* would not have the knowledge of Arab society to put the passage in its proper context. The two Western women shoppers—one European and one American—speak a total of eight languages. Ironically, none of the eight is Arabic. Uris condemns his own straw man: "The Arab was versed only in Arabic" (p. 376). For an American to speak three languages is highly unusual. It is, of course, almost unheard of for an urban merchant in the Middle East to speak only one. The purpose of the entire passage is to underscore the greed, stupidity and unattractiveness of the Arab merchant.

Nor does the narrative include any positively drawn Arab characters to counter the negative ones. Indeed, everywhere there are repeated references to Arab slave markets, white slavery, hashish users and Arab thugs and gangsters (pp. 31, 467, 213, 274-75). There are no happy Arab families or honest, heroic Arab characters in the novel. Uris consistently emphasizes the alleged corruption of Arab society. In fact, the data on the Arabs reveal a quite different picture. Even after World War II, the Arab world was still highly traditional, rural and family oriented. Crime, as known in the West, was exceedingly rare and was generally confined to a few urban areas such as Cairo. Notably, drug and alcohol use (the latter being specifically prohibited in Islam) and other social crimes were treated much more harshly under Arab nationalist leaders such as Nasser than they often had been under imperial, Western controls.

Along with its obvious anti-Arab racism, the novel is also blatantly sexist regarding Arab women, who are described as both repressed and treacherous. In one passage Arab women are characterized as seeking "revenge by dagger or poison" (p. 229). Later some Christian Arabs seek to sell their virgin sister (p. 334). The plots of popular novels often focus simultaneously on the alleged mistreatment of women in the Arab world and on the provocative, cunning nature of Arab women. The juxtaposition of contradictory traits, in this case submission and treachery, has already been noted as a technique common in racist and sexist propaganda.

The role of women in Islamic and Arab society has been widely maligned and misunderstood. Westerners have consistently sought to describe Arab society in light of their own preconceived prejudices. However, a great deal of scholarly work has been published on the role of women in the Middle East.[11] Although Arab women, like their Western sisters, are victimized by male chauvinism and prejudice, they are by no means as subjugated or oppressed as most Western popular literature would indicate. Women's roles in Arab society vary greatly and reflect the geographic, economic and social complexity of the society at large. It is also important to emphasize that women were extremely active in the Arab nationalist, anti-imperialist movements of the twentieth century. Indeed, in Egypt, Algeria and elsewhere, women were often in the vanguard of political demonstrations and led the way for social reforms.

The portrayal of Arabs as irrational and mysterious figures is common in *Exodus*. Jewish refugees into Palestine are given courses on "Arab psychology" (pp. 38, 229), for the Western characters perceive Arab behavior as senseless. According to Uris their very language reflects this chaos. Arabic and Arabs remain inexplicable to outsiders (p. 229). In contrast, Hebrew, although, like Arabic, a Semitic language, is described as logical (p. 53). The supposed "irrationality" of Arabs, and by extension of all Third World peoples, in contrast to the so-called rationality of the Western world, is an underlying assumption in much Western writing.

This preconception of the irrationality and inferiority of the Arab world is closely correlated with the denigration of Arab

---

[11]*Middle Eastern Muslim Women Speak*, ed. Elizabeth Warnock Fernea and Basima Qattan Bezirgan, Austin: University of Texas Press, 1977, is an excellent example of a thoughtful, scholarly study of women in the Middle East.

culture and civilization. Sweeping critical generalizations regarding Arab culture are commonly found in popular literature. For example, in *Exodus* Arab civilization is described as having collapsed after the Crusades (p. 227). Toward the end of *Exodus* there is a passage that itemizes five of the basic components that make up the popular Western image of the Arab world. In order to analyze and refute these five misconceptions it is instructive to look at this short passage in greater detail. Uris summarizes all of Arab society in the following sweeping terms:

> . . . *There was little song or laughter or joy in Arab life. It was a constant struggle to survive.*
>
> *In this atmosphere cunning, treachery, murder, feuds, and jealousies became a way of life. The cruel realities that had gone into forming the Arab character puzzled outsiders.*
>
> *Cruelty from brother to brother was common. . . . There was little compassion from Arab to Arab. The* fellaheen *who lived in abysmal filth and the Bedouin whose survival was a day-to-day miracle turned to the one means of alleviating their misery. They became Muslim fanatics as elements of the Jews had become fanatics in their hour of distress.*
>
> *It was small wonder that the Arabs mistrusted all outsiders. The restless movement for freedom originated with the ruling classes, for the Bedouins and* fellaheen *were far too demoralized even to comprehend freedom and better conditions. The masses were but pawns in the schemes of the effendis and sheikhs. They could be stirred into religious hysteria at the least provocation and were thus useful as a political weapon* (p. 228).

This apparently didactic description of Arab society is replete with breathtaking social and historical distortions. Indeed, in order to have such massive generalizations accepted by the reader, the author must rely on the ignorance of the average Westerner as to the real nature and complexity of Arab society. Hence, in the first of these basic misrepresentations, Uris can casually argue that history and culture have contrived to make the Arabs a violent people. The theme of the Arabs as more violent than other national or ethnic groups appears repeatedly in *Exodus* and the Western media in general. *Exodus* is replete with violent Arab figures. The riots in Palestine during the nineteen-twenties and thirties are described as times when Arabs rampaged through Jewish quarters "with murder, rape, and plunder in their hearts" (p. 466). Earlier in the narrative a Zionist settler summarizes the Arab character in the following terms: "One thing an Arab understands"—and he held up his fist and shook it—"he understands this" (pp. 224-25). In one sweeping gesture the entire Arab world has been branded as understanding only force. The message delivered by *Exodus* is that Arabs as a group (or race) are *inherently* violent. As has been noted, the close juxtaposition of racial prejudice and the imputation that the out-group, in this case Arabs, is violent *by nature* has been consistently emphasized and refuted in studies dealing with prejudice.

Secondly, this violent nature is purportedly evident throughout Arab family and interpersonal relationships. Ari, the leading Zionist protagonist in *Exodus* accuses one Palestinian Arab of refusing to face the truth that, ". . . no one hates or exploits an Arab worse than another Arab" (p. 344). In a travesty of well-documented anthropological and sociological evidence regarding the close familial and loyal personal relations enjoyed in most Arab society, Arab interpersonal relations in *Exodus* are condemned as joyless and full of treachery.

In *The Haj* (1985), which reads much like a five-hundred-page anti-Arab diatribe, Uris expands on this theme. In contrast to *Exodus*, in *The Haj* Arabs are the central characters. The plot revolves around the ultimate destruction of Haj Ibrahim Al-Soukori, a *mukhtar* (mayor) of the Palestinian village of Tabah, and his family. For Uris there is absolutely nothing positive about this Palestinian village or the entire Arab world. Arabs are depicted in *The Haj* as incapable of loving relationships, having no technical skills, no compassion, not even any toys! All of these allegations are examples of either Uris's narrow knowledge or his deliberate misrepresentation of Arab and Islamic culture. For instance, toys have a long history in the Arab world. It is well-known, in the Muslim world at least, that even the Prophet Muhammad's favorite wife Aisha owned dolls.

Arabs in *The Haj*—as in *Exodus*—are uniformly portrayed in the crudest and most venial terms. The Arab world (its history, politics, social structures) are condemned through the voices and eyes of the Arab characters themselves.

Although there are many scholarly studies that refute the erroneous picture painted by Uris in both *Exodus* and *The Haj*, the anthology *Peoples and Cultures of the Middle East*, edited by Louise Sweet, is one of the best studies on Arab society. The second volume focuses on family and personal life in Arab cities, towns and the countryside and documents the reciprocal, highly interdependent nature of the society.[12]

Third, Arab society is seen as hopelessly backward and stagnant. Arabs are characterized as dirty and poor. In *Exodus*, "dirty little Arab children" (p. 348) are helped by the American nurse. Even when brought to them by an Arab doctor, modern medicine remains a threat to primitive and illiterate villagers (p. 226). In popular novels technology and science are alien to Arabs. One Arab landlord in *Exodus* sells his land to the Zionist settlers because he admires their advanced farming techniques (pp. 260-61). The implication is that Arab landlords never had the know-how or ability to apply similar methods. Of course, this image is directly correlated to the perpetuation of the "barren desert" myth that has been discussed previously. The rapid technological development of much of the Arab world in the past twenty years indicates that Arab society was eager and able to make scientific and developmental gains, but that it wished to do so on its own terms and not under Western domination.

Not only does the emphasis on the backwardness of Arab society present a highly misleading picture, the impression is based on an even more questionable assumption. In these passages, the concept of "modern" is equated with that which is "Western";

---

[12]Louise E. Sweet, ed., *Peoples and Cultures of the Middle East*, 2 vol., New York: The Natural History Press, 1970. *Man, State, and Society in the Contemporary Middle East*, Jacob M. Landau, ed., New York: Praeger, 1972, provides another overview.

furthermore, it is assumed that "Western" is both rational and desirable. Not to desire the modern or Western is to be irrational and backward. The plots in *Exodus* and in later popular fiction have often been based on the premise that the creation of a Zionist nation in the Middle East was desirable, not only for humanitarian reasons, but because it would result in the Westernization of the area. In keeping with the refusal to recognize their existence, Palestinian Arabs are not specifically mentioned. That Arabs in general opposed the creation of a Zionist or Western nation in their midst was, *ipso facto*, proof of their irrationality.

Fourth, bad leadership is depicted as virtually the rule throughout the Arab world. Nasser, who was a genuinely popular Arab leader, is dismissed by Uris as a Hitler. In novels written after the advent of wealth from petroleum resources, the Arab world is described as being controlled by a few oil-rich sheikhs. In the popular rendition, sheikhs indulge themselves in an orgy of conspicuous consumption while the Arab masses remain in degradation. In *Exodus*, Arab leaders are described as corrupt, scheming, venial and brutal. The Arab world as a whole is also accused of discouraging good leadership. Toward the end of the novel, one Israeli character summarizes the attitude of the Arab world toward its leaders:

> *Unfortunately, whenever an enlightened Arab leader arises he is generally murdered. The Arabs want neither resettlement of the refugees, alleviation of their plight, nor do they want peace* (p. 554).

This image of corrupt leadership and irrational, violent people persists in much popular writing. The massive development projects implemented by many Arab governments and the progressive societal changes of the recent past have not found their way into that medium.

Fifth, through innuendo and distortion, the entire Arab national movement is discredited. Whereas Zionism or Jewish nationalism is glorified as a legitimate historical movement based upon the national revival of the Jewish people, Arab nationalism is consistently denigrated. Arabs are depicted as having little real attachment to the land. The departure of numerous Palestinian Arabs during the 1948 war is offered as proof of this lack of commitment.

> *If the Arabs of Palestine loved their land, they could not have been forced from it—much less run from it without real cause. The Arabs had little to live for, much less to fight for. This is not the reaction of a man who loves his land* (p. 554).

In *Exodus* Arab nationalism is portrayed as the creation of landowners and self-serving leaders. Through the manipulation of Arab nationalism, the Arab masses have become pawns for the personal ambitions of their corrupt leaders and for the imperial policies of the British. The novel leaves the reader with the impression that the Arab masses were duped into believing in Arab nationalism. Arab nationalism—as described in *Exodus*—is not an indigenous movement; it is not credited as a legitimate expression of self-determination, but rather as a chimera. Because of its artificial nature, Arab nationalism has, according to the narrative, "degenerated into a hate-filled dogma" (p. 224). Actually, Arab nationalism, like all Third World national movements, had its roots in the genuine desire of the masses for independence from imperial domination. The close ties of Israel with the West and the geopolitical interests of the United States and the Soviet Union have often impeded Arab demands for independence. In addition, the strategic location of the vast petroleum reserves of the Arab world have put the region in the forefront of competition between the super-powers. In *Exodus*, these complex issues are not mentioned, let alone explained.

Rather, Uris portrays the purported bankruptcy of Arab nationalism, the backwardness of the society, and the corruption of their leaders, as having caused the Arab masses to become religious fanatics. References to Arab or Muslim mobs and "wild chanting" (p. 421) are common. The religious fanaticism of Arabs and the Muslim world in general is one of the major themes in popular novels. This theme, evident in *Exodus*, will be amplified and exaggerated by innumerable Western writers. As explicated by Edward Said in *Covering Islam* and Godfrey Jansen in *Militant Islam*, the

Western world has historically viewed Islam as a threat and has reinforced negative images of Islam over many centuries. The current movement in the Middle East toward a renaissance of Islamic government has attracted widespread attention. Within large portions of Arab society these movements are perceived as a means to counter and possibly to eclipse Western domination—whether political, military, cultural or economic. However, it is vital to recall that the Islamic world is one of great diversity, and to treat it as a monolithic enemy, as is so often done in popular writing, is both erroneous and counterproductive.

Exodus is a prime example of a novel in which virtually every aspect of the Arab world—its people, history, culture and religion—is criticized in the most sweeping and distorted generalizations. The novel contains all of the stereotypes and misrepresentations of the Arabs that the Western world has traditionally held. The composite picture given in *Exodus* is unremittingly positive toward Israel and equally consistent in its hostility toward the Arabs. In *Exodus* Uris has defined Israel, the history of the entire Middle East and the Arab-Israeli conflict in purely Zionist terms. He does not make any reference or give consideration to conflicting viewpoints or to historical facts that contradict his interpretation.

The impact of *Exodus* on the general public and on other writers of popular fiction dealing with the Middle East needs little reiteration. Louis L'Amour's *The Walking Drum* is perhaps the sole recent bestselling novel that describes the Arab world and its contributions to civilization in positive and historically accurate detail. Although the novel is set almost entirely in the Arab world and most of its characters are Arabs, the advertisements and cover for the book give no indication of its Middle Eastern theme. Best known for his popular novels on the American West, L'Amour notes that he has been fascinated with the 12th century, the Golden Age of Islam, and plans several more adventures based on Kerbouchard, the hero in *The Walking Drum*.

However, L'Amour's approach is the exception. Many more authors, including James Michener and Clive Irving, have continually repeated and expanded the historical myths and anti-Arab attitudes that pervaded *Exodus* in their own widely publicized novels on the creation of Israel. In the absence of any contravening evidence or depictions in popular literature or the media in general, the bulk of Western society accepted the interpretation as given in *Exodus* at face value. As the following chapters will demonstrate, successive generations of novelists and writers of popular literature have, with a few notable exceptions, perpetuated this pattern.

III. BIOGRAPHICAL WORKS

Autobiographies by well-known Israeli leaders such as Golda Meir, Moshe Dayan and Ezer Weizman have been particularly successful in popular book markets. By 1979 Golda Meir's *My Life* was in its fifth paperback printing. Her life story was subsequently made into a television docu-drama starring the award-winning actress Ingrid Bergman. In a common advertising technique, the covers of these autobiographies often highlight excerpts from favorable reviews. For example, the cover of Meir's *My Life* included a statement from the world-renowned evangelist Billy Graham, who reputedly commented that it was "about the greatest book I have ever read."[1] Similarly, the cover of Dayan's *Story of My Life* featured excerpts from *Newsweek* and the *New York Times Book Review*; in addition, Dayan's book was a Jewish Book Club and alternate Book-of-the-Month Club selection. Hence these books were both widely publicized and distributed.

As a rule, authors of autobiographies and biographies make their viewpoints and prejudices evident from the outset. Not suprisingly, Golda Meir, Moshe Dayan, Menachem Begin and Ezer Weizman all clearly support Zionism and paint an almost totally positive picture of Israeli policy and actions.[2] Although Golda Meir in *My Life* and Moshe Dayan in *Story of My Life* both write preceptively and movingly of Israel, they reveal a myopia regarding the Palestinian Arabs who lived on the land the Zionists claim. For Meir, as for the many other Israelis who have written their autobiographies, the Jewish claim to Palestine is morally and religiously superior to all others.

---

[1]Golda Meir, *My Life*, back cover of Dell paperback edition.
[2]Golda Meir, *op. cit.;* Moshe Dayan, *Moshe Dayan: Story of My Life*, New York: Warner Books, 1977; Menachem Begin, *The Revolt*, New York: 1948, 2nd. ed., Nash Publishing, 1972, Dell, 1977; Ezer Weizman, *On Eagles' Wings*, New York: Macmillan, 1976.

Understandably, the Holocaust had a shattering, traumatic impact upon all Jewish communities. For Meir the tragedy strongly reinforced Zionist demands for the establishment of a Jewish state in Palestine. For the Zionists, the Holocaust was the final justification for a Jewish state that would be a safe haven from the "inherent" anti-Semitism of Western civilization. The suffering and decimation of European Jewry was, for Meir and other Zionists, the ultimate argument in favor of Jewish rights to the land of Palestine. Any other nationalist movement, however legitimate, paled before their own overwhelming claims. These claims were based not only upon religious injunctions regarding Israel as the chosen land for the chosen people, but were legitimized by the age-old persecution and suffering of the Jews in the West.

In their statements aimed for the Western world, the Zionists constantly strove to reinforce the guilt Western society rightfully felt over the horrors perpetrated by the Nazis. However, as the plight of the European Jews has been emphasized, the suffering of countless others—leftists, gypsies, Slavs—has been obscured or made to look relatively unimportant. Similarly, the suffering of the Palestinian Arabs has been largely ignored, denied, or obfuscated. This denial has continued in spite of the fact that before the creation of Israel in 1948 the Palestinians comprised two-thirds of the local population in Palestine, owned most of the land and had clear-cut rights based upon long-term historical possession of the territory. However, Meir, like her mentor, David Ben-Gurion, argues that the most important consideration for Israeli leaders has always been, "In the long run, is it good for the state?" Meir has no difficulty in justifying the apparent extension of the olive branch while retaliating against any "gangs of Arab infiltrators."[3] Meir never recognizes the Palestinians as a national entity; as a result she never deals philosophically or politically with their national aspirations. For Meir, an old guard Zionist, the Jews have the right to the land. Any attempts by Arabs or others to alter or to question that claim threatened Israel and had to be opposed

---

[3]*Ibid.*, p. 274.

BIOGRAPHICAL WORKS

with all the forces (military, economic, political, moral) that the state could bring to bear.

The view has remained unchanged since the inception of the Zionist movement. Meir's attitude toward Palestinians, whom she avoids mentioning by name, remained constant from her arrival in Palestine in 1921 to her death in 1978. The Palestinian opponents or "gangs" of the 1920s and 1930s became the "terrorists" of the 1960s and 1970s. For Meir, both are to be fought and removed from the Israeli nation. In her autobiography she never considers the deeper causes for the Palestinian opposition.

In *My Life* the Arabs are clearly the out-group. Like other Zionists raised with Western stereotypes of the Oriental world, Meir regards Arabs as somehow lesser personalities. In these first-hand Zionist narratives, Arabs seem to live in a shadowy world populated by terrorists and cowards. Writing for a Western audience, Meir notes that "assassination is an endemic disease in the Arab world," that Arabs "kill and destroy," and that, in the opinion of one leading Israeli, the "Bedouin had their own ideas about truth—which they saw as something much less absolute than we did" (p. 207). In the same manner, Richard and Irving Greenfield in *The Life of Menachem Begin* refer to Arabs as "terrorists" or "murderers."⁴ As in *Exodus* these descriptions of Arabs parallel the racial stereotypes of blacks in the United States and of Algerians under French colonialism. Nowhere do the authors of these biographical accounts question the origins or validity of these biases.

In contrast, these biographical accounts gloss over Zionist and Israeli terrorist activities. Indeed, the paperback cover of Begin's *The Revolt* proudly describes him as "commanding a daring band of Israeli Freedom Fighters." These "Freedom Fighters" were, of course, the well-known Irgun Zvai Leumi, which was responsible for the April 1948 attack on the Palestinian village of Deir Yassin where approximately 250 civilians were massacred. Another

---

⁴*Ibid.*, p. 206. Richard Pierce Greenfield and Irving A. Greenfield, *The Life Story of Menachem Begin*, New York: Manor Books, 1977.

Irgun member, Abraham Stern, was the founder of the even more extreme *Lochamei Herut Israel* (LEHI) or "Stern Gang." Itzhak Shamir, who ultimately became a prime minister of Israel, was a member of the Stern Gang and one of Begin's political confidants. The Stern was responsible for the assassinations of Lord Moyne, British Colonial Secretary, in 1944, and Count Bernadotte, the Swedish United Nations mediator, in 1948. However, the Zionist use of terrorism is usually ignored in popular biographies.

Similarly, in her descriptions of the 1956, 1967 and 1973 Arab-Israeli wars, Meir vindicates all Israeli actions, even those which contributed to escalating the conflicts. She assumes, probably correctly, that her Western readers already consider Israel the underdog who through perseverance and moral right has triumphed against enormous odds. Meir dismisses any Israeli responsibility for the wars and for the Palestinian refugees.

> The "Palestinian refugees" [the diacritical marks are Meir's] were created as a result of the Arab desire (and attempt) to destroy Israel. . . . Of course, there were some Jews in the Yishuv who said, even in 1948, that the Arab exodus was the best thing that could have happened to Israel, but I know of no serious Israeli who ever felt that way (p. 269).

In the latter, Meir chooses to ignore public statements by Zionists of the stature of Moshe Dayan and Menachem Begin, both of whom have stated that the exodus of Palestinians considerably aided the establishment of a Jewish state. Meir, a sophisticated politician, could hardly have been so ingenuous as to be unaware of these opinions.

Meir's book and biographies such as Robert Slater's *Golda: The Uncrowned Queen of Israel* have reinforced Western perceptions of Israel as a beleaguered nation that has done its best to achieve peace and justice in spite of irrational, virulent Arab opposition. The persistence of Palestinian/Arab opposition is not taken as evidence of a legitimate grievance. Arab opposition is perceived as further evidence of the old stereotypes of Arabs as irrational and essentially violent people.

The recent publications on Menachem Begin's life offer further examples of this approach. The incongruities between Begin's activities as leader of the Irgun, which perpetrated terrorist attacks upon the British and the Palestinian Arabs prior to 1948, and his steadfast refusal to recognize, let alone to negotiate with, the Palestinians, whom Begin characterizes as "terrorists" and "murderers," are clear to anyone familiar with the history of Israel. However, publications like Richard and Irving Greenfield's *The Life Story of Menachem Begin* ignore this basic inconsistency. The Greenfield book is in no way comparable to the in-depth autobiography by Meir. Its treatment of Begin's life is, at best, cursory. There is no table of contents or index. The narrative provides scant information on Begin's childhood and virtually omits reference to his schooling. It does, however, include a great deal of extraneous material regarding Jewish history under the Romans. The authors neglect to mention when Begin arrived in Palestine, nor do they discuss his activities as leader and tactician of the Irgun. The narrative also contains many gaps regarding Begin's political, marital and familial history.

Ironically, Begin himself displays no such hesitancy about his past in his autobiography. *The Revolt* was originally published in Hebrew with an English translation in 1948; following Begin's election as prime minister of Israel, it was reissued in 1977. *The Revolt* is a full, if self-serving, account of Irgun activities prior to and immediately following the creation of Israel. In it Begin clearly elucidates his fundamental belief in Zionism as the legitimate expression of Jewish nationalism and in his commitment to the establishment of a Jewish state over all of "Eretz Israel," including what he calls Judea and Samaria. Begin is militant in his desire for the realization of Israeli domination of all the territory given by God to the ancient Hebrews. For him, participation in the Irgun was the logical outgrowth of those beliefs. For Begin and many others, the massacre at Deir Yassin and other terrorist acts perpetrated by the Irgun and the Stern are fully justified because the use of force was necessary to secure a Jewish state. In the words of Ivan M. Greenberg, the editor of *The Revolt*, Begin "probably more than any single one of his contemporaries was responsible for the emergence of the sovereign Jewish State of Israel.''[5] This theme was obviously echoed by the many Israelis who supported Begin's political parties and who twice elected him prime minister of Israel.

It is outside the scope of this study to argue the relative merits of terrorism. However it is pertinent to emphasize the discrepancy between the acceptance and glorification of Zionist terrorism and the condemnation of the use of terrorist tactics by Palestinians and other Arabs. At various times in the conflict, both Israelis and Palestinians have, out of desperation, ideological commitment and military considerations adopted terrorism as a tactic to further their national aspirations. The fact that historically *both* sides have used terrorism has not been conveyed to readers of popular books or, indeed, to the Western public in general. Consequently, in popular writing Israeli terrorism has been portrayed as the struggle of freedom fighters or as necessary for a national cause, while Palestinian or Arab use of the same tactics has been condemned as inhumane and barbaric. Begin also makes no secret of his disdain for the political pragmatism of Ben-Gurion and his followers. Begin's biographers, like the Greenfields, are considerably more discreet about his stormy relations with leaders of the Labor Party. Israeli politicians clearly have had differing tactical views on how to implement the best interests of the state. They may also continue to differ over the exact boundaries for the state, but they remain understandably united in their determination to do whatever is best for the continued survival and prosperity of Israel.

Consequently, the treatment of the Palestinian issue is the same in all of these biographical works. Generally, Palestinian Arabs as a separate entity from the larger Arab world are not mentioned. Arabs are viewed collectively as a threat to the State of Israel. As in Meir's account, Begin and the Greenfields reject Israeli responsibility for the refugees. That the Irgun attacks on villages helped to incite a large-scale Palestinian exodus is not considered. In an

---

[5]Menachem Begin, *The Revolt*, New York: Dell, 1977, p. 9.

attempt to exonerate the Irgun for its attack on Deir Yassin, the Greenfields depict the village as an important military site. They argue that the Irgun attack shocked Begin. Begin's own rendition in *The Revolt* does not indicate shock. In the aftermath he attempts to vindicate the Irgun's philosophy that force was absolutely necessary in order to establish a Jewish state. In spite of Begin's forthright justification of the use of force, the Greenfields describe Deir Yassin as "the one ugly note in an incredible saga of heroism and military accomplishment."[6] Begin and the Irgun are depicted as freedom fighters seeking to establish a democratic state. The Palestinian Arabs, with similar national aspirations, are characterized as terrorists without any legitimate goals. The theme that the Israelis fight on the side of moral right and that the Palestinians seek only to destroy pervades all of these biographies. In publications such as the Greenfield study of Begin, the biases are clearly apparent. Indeed, the Greenfields make no attempt to present an objective or even-handed treatment of Begin. Their work is clearly intended as a panegyric.

Other personal accounts, such as Saul Bellow's *To Jerusalem and Back,* attempt, at least superficially, to present a more balanced rendition. Written and published immediately following Bellow's acceptance of the Nobel Prize in literature, *To Jerusalem and Back* is Bellow's description of his emotional and intellectual impressions of Israel. Many of the views expressed by Bellow were echoed by Barbara Tuchman in a July 25, 1982, *New York Times* article. Both pieces clearly illustrate the common assumptions and attitudes regarding the Middle East that are held by many contemporary authors. Justifiably renowned for the literary skills and sensitivity they have brought to innumerable other topics, Bellow and Tuchman reveal a marked bias regarding the Middle East.

Bellow's descriptions of Israel depict a landscape perceived by a Western Jew who has been imbued with a whole body of religious and ethnic memories. As with other writers conveying travel expe-

---

[6] Greenfields, p. 203.

riences, Bellow tends to notice and describe the "exotic," the different, or those aspects of Israel that seem related to his own Western experiences. He, too, tends to categorize the Palestinians under the catchall label "the Arabs."

In an amazing manipulation of moral rectitude, particularly for one of his literary sensitivity, Bellow justifies Israeli actions in the following terms:

Such injustices as have been committed against the Arabs can be more readily justified by Judaism, by the whole of Jewish history, than by Zionism alone.[7]

Bellow has returned to the premises of Ben-Gurion and Meir. Judaism and the mere fact of being Jewish have given the Israelis and the Israeli state special exemption. The theme of "chosenness" or higher national claims echoes through much Zionist writing. The Israeli author Amos Elon has reiterated both the attitude of superior claims and the ignorance of the Arab situation held by many early Zionists in his fine biography of Theodor Herzl, one of the founding fathers of the movement.[8] The implication of national superiority, whether fully elucidated or not, carries with it an inherent logic of racial superiority. The Holocaust reinforced and intensified the attitude of special claims held by the early Zionists.

Although Bellow reluctantly admits that the Israelis might have done more to aid the Palestinian refugees, he concludes that since "what the Nazis had done to the Jew (in no way) resembled what Zionism had done to the Arabs—a parallel no sane person would agree to" (p. 122), there was no cause for Israeli guilt or responsibility. Going to an even greater extreme to absolve the Israelis, Tuchman argues that the problems of the refugees and, indeed, the entire conflict, have been caused by "Arab intransigence" and, being Arab problems, must be solved solely by the Arabs.

---

[7]Saul Bellow, *To Jerusalem and Back: a Personal Account*, New York: Viking Press, 1976; Penguin, 1977, p. 54.

[8]Amos Elon, *Herzl*, New York: Holt, Rinehard and Winston, 1975.

Bellow also exonerates the Israelis because of their creativity and moral superiority. Having assumed the creative superiority of Israel, Bellow proceeds to argue that Israel represents a dynamic force, not only in the Middle East, but throughout the world. In support of this stance he cites Mikhail Agursky, a writer from the Soviet Union now living in Israel.

> . . . I am advocating such an objective—to make Israel the center of the new civilization . . . taking into consideration the evident decline of the Western (and Eastern as well) civilization (pp. 80-81).

In one sweep of the pen, Bellow concurs that Western and Eastern civilizations have reached their apogees, and that Israel represents the best possible redemption.

Having posited the case for Israeli superiority, Bellow, in opposition to other Western intellectuals such as Jean Paul Sartre, opines that Western thinkers ought to have the moral courage to ask Islamic society to make adjustments for Israel. Although sympathetic to Israel, Sartre also made a case for the historical reality of Palestinian Arab national rights. In addition to calling for revolution in the Arab world, he attempted—without success—to institute a dialogue between Israelis and Arabs.[9] Bellow continues that "a great civilization should be capable of humane and generous flexibility" (p. 128). The Arab refusal to accept Israel therefore appears to indicate that it is neither great nor humane. On the other hand, Bellow depicts Israel as "too small and too special" (p. 141) to be compared to other nations.

For Bellow, Israel "stands for something in Western history" (p. 157). Worried over the future of democracy in Israel, Bellow warns against the possible Levantization of the state. The latter is a recurrent leitmotif in Zionist writings including those of Moshe Dayan and Abba Eban. In this context "Levantization" means becoming part of the Arab world; the root of the term is based on the imperial-geographic concept of the Levant or that part of the

---

[9]See *Les Temps Modernes* (Special Issue), "Le Conflit Israélo-Arabe" (June 1967), for a fuller exposition of Sartre's position.

eastern Mediterranean which under the Ottoman empire had formed the coastal region of Greater Syria. The term "Levantization" implies not only absorption into the geographic region, but social, economic and cultural assimilation as well. Israeli leaders have consistently warned against such assimilation. Abba Eban elucidated this point in his book, *My Country*:

> *Some writers, despairing of any Arab reconciliation with a "Zionist" Israel, have drawn false comfort from the prospect that Israel might become increasingly orientalized until it loses the qualities which separate it from the rest of the Middle East and becomes absorbed unobtrusively in the surrounding Levantine region. There is no chance of this coming to pass. Israel will always be non-Arab in its speech, thought and shape of mind; and its Jewish connections will always be stronger than anything else.*[10]

Moshe Dayan summarized the Israeli position on the television show *Face the Nation* on June 11, 1967, shortly after the Israeli victory in the 1967 war. When asked whether Israel could absorb the large numbers of Arabs under Israeli occupation, Dayan replied:

> *Economically we can; but I think that is not in accord with our aims in the future. It would turn Israel into either a bi-national or poly-Arab-Jewish state, and we want to have a Jewish state. We can absorb them, but then it won't be the same country. . . . We want a Jewish state like the French have a French state.*[11]

Bellow apparently agrees with Elie Kedourie, a well-known professor of Arab history, with whom he speaks in London. Kedourie and others have stressed that the Arab world has been controlled largely by "fervent Muslims, whose thought has been least influenced by Western ideas" (p. 143). They are least likely to accept Israel. In the role of a Western liberal, Bellow, perhaps ingenuously, asks if there are no Arab intellectuals who would "disassociate themselves . . . from the traditional religious patriotism." Kedourie replies, "It is useless to apply our Western measures and expectations to Arab intellectuals" (p. 144).

---

[10]Abba Eban, *My Country*, New York: Random House, 1972, p. 286.
[11]Moshe Dayan, *Face the Nation*, June 11, 1967.

Bellow does not acknowledge, let alone discuss, the possible similarities between alleged Arab "religious patriotism" and what might well be referred to as the "religious patriotism" in Israel. In almost every sphere of Israeli life, religious coalitions play an important role. Religious groups have demanded and received considerations in formulating laws, particularly those governing social matters such as marriage and divorce. Under the multi-party political system, religious blocs have been instrumental in formulating and bringing down successive Israeli governments. "Religious patriots" have also been the vanguard of the movement to settle and to claim the West Bank and other territory as part of Israel's national patrimony.

According to the narrative, after Bellow returned to the United States, he continued to seek clarification regarding the Arab-Israeli conflict. Having accepted Zionism and the inferiority of Arab national claims, Bellow fails to understand why the Arabs persist in their opposition. He asks Professor Yehoshafat Harkabi for explanations. Harkabi is one of Israel's foremost tacticians, a former intelligence officer, and a writer on Palestinian commando movements. Not surprisingly, Harkabi reiterates that Westerners and Israelis (as fellow Westerners) do not understand the Arab mentality. Harkabi notes that in his opinion during the Mandate period "the Palestinian Arabs gave little evidence of being particularly attached to the country" (p. 151) and that many sold land to the Zionists. In few other instances has the sale of land meant the negation of national rights, but Harkabi insists upon the Israeli right to the land. This stance reflects the position taken by Uris in *Exodus* and again ignores the historical fact that the Palestinian Arabs continued to own the majority of the land throughout the entire time of the Mandate.

Bellow also seeks to undercut so-called "Arabist" objections to the view that Israel has the right to the land. In an ironical, although certainly unintentional twist, Bellow criticizes Arabs who proclaim that Westerners are too simplistic to understand the Arab world. Yet both Bellow and the so-called "Arabists," or Orientalists, as Edward Said has called them in *Orientalism*, simplistically label all Arabs as alien outsiders. Both Bellow and Tuchman are thoroughly critical of Islam and Arab history and civilization. Both ignore the religious heterogeneity and historical tolerance of the Arab world. Bellow belittles its "traditional religious patriotism" and Tuchman writes about holy wars. Islam is criticized simultaneously as backward and as threatening to Western/Christian hegemony. Arab nations are depicted as retrograde and quarrelsome. Completely distorting the reality of the Arab world, Tuchman rhetorically asks what Arab nations have done other than to "quarrel and fight, build skyscraper cities in the desert and ludicrously enrich their sheikhs." In a description based largely upon a simplistic interpretation of Malcolm Kerr's *The Arab Cold War*, Bellow disparages the political infighting among the Arabs. Bellow's comments do not indicate the subtlety of Kerr's short study. *The Arab-Cold War* delinates the nature of intra-Arab politics from 1958 to 1964 much as other studies have explained the interrelationships among European nations or the Cold War between the superpowers.

Bellow and Tuchman blame the Arab world and "its" Soviet ally for the mounting violence in the region. Neither writer notes that the Soviets did not play a role in the Arab world until the Western nations, particularly the United States, had persistently supported Israel. Nor do they indicate the role of the United States in attempting to force the Arab world away from a neutral role in the Cold War and into direct alliance with the West. In addition to using anti-Arab and anti-Islamic motifs, Tuchman and many other contemporary writers warn against OPEC and Arab control of their own petroleum resources. Tuchman describes OPEC as "holding its Western customers in pitiful thrall."

When OPEC was formed in 1959, Western companies had controlled petroleum exploration, concession contracts, prices and distribution for over fifty years. As is well known among oil industry analysts, Venezuela, Iran and other non-Arab countries—not the Arab states—were the leaders in coordinating the efforts of the oil-exporting nations to obtain a greater share of the benefits from this major resource. OPEC did not become effective in forcing a redistribution of petroleum profits until the 1970s.

To Jerusalem and Back was written prior to the Camp David accords, the Egyptian-Israeli peace treaty and the 1982 Israeli invasion of Lebanon. However, toward the end of the book, Bellow recounts an exchange between himself and Morris Janowitz, a well-known specialist on the Israeli military and society. At that time Janowitz made the prescient observation that although Israel would certainly win a future military confrontation, another round would have huge human costs and would result in a severe trauma within Israeli society. Bellow wrongly concluded that it would be the Arabs who would reject all Israeli peace initiatives and that it would be the Arabs who would engage in violence in Lebanon. Bellow ends on the woeful note that in the modern Middle East ". . . the eagerness to kill for political ends—or to justify killing by such ends—is as keen now as it ever was" (p. 182). The reader is left with the impression that for Bellow, as for countless others, the confict will continue unabated as Israel strives for peace and the Arabs persist in their opposition. Bellow did not foresee or anticipate that Egypt would take the initiative toward direct negotiations and that Israel would considerably escalate the level of violence with its 1982 invasion of Lebanon.

Bellow and Tuchman are not the first or only writers to devise or to enunciate anti-Arab, anti-Islamic and anti-OPEC sentiments. However, that writers of their intellectual abilities should perpetuate these stereotypes without questioning their origins or validity indicates the pervasiveness of negative Western attitudes toward the Arab world. Thus it is not surprising that writers of considerably less distinction and literary reputation commonly use these same negative images.

The previously mentioned biographical works represent a small fraction of the popular publications devoted to Israeli leaders. These biographies give the Western audience highly personalized pictures of Israelis and some idea of the complex Israeli political scene. More important, these works reinforce support for Israel and hostility toward the Arab world. In contrast, there are very few popular biographies of Arab leaders; the few works that focus on Arabs are often openly hostile.

For example, *Carlos: Terror International* by Dennis Eisenberg and Eli Landau[12] and published by Corgi, is extremely negative on the subject of Arab Palestinians. While treating the ideological motivations of Carlos' associates (Carlos being the elusive international assassin, presumably from Venezuela) in the most superficial manner, the authors stress the unpleasant characteristics and sexual exploits of Carlos.

Likewise, Thomas Kiernan in *Yasir Arafat* devotes over two hundred pages to Arafat's childhood and early manhood; he dismisses the crucial decade from 1967 to 1978 in a scant nine pages. Consequently, the entire time frame during which Arafat and the Palestinian struggle attracted global attention is given no more than a cursory glance. Although he initially notes that a historical perspective is necessary to understanding Arafat, Kiernan omits the political background that led to Arafat's emergence as leader of the Palestine Liberation Organization (PLO). Nor does he treat the vital splits among the Palestinian leadership or Arafat's pragmatic politics, which have caused some Palestinians to eschew his leadership. How Arafat has managed to remain the major leader of the PLO in spite of these internal conflicts is not discussed.

These matters are crucial to an understanding not only of Arafat, but of the entire Palestinian national movement. Rather than deal with these vital issues, Kiernan gives the reader a scenario of Arafat's early life. Kiernan concludes, after innumerable stories about Arafat's birth, that he was born in Egypt, thereby implying that Arafat is not Palestinian. Emphasizing Arafat's kinship with the Husseini family, Kiernan proceeds to trace Arafat's unhappy childhood, which was punctuated with family problems and mounting political violence in Egypt. As sources, Kiernan generally uses unidentified eye-witnesses. Kiernan also includes the

---

[12]Dennis Eisenberg and Eli Landau, *Carlos: Terror International*, London: Corgi, 1976.

types of sexual innuendoes and slander about Arabs which have been noted in other works. In short, Kiernan concludes that most of Arafat's reputation is based upon myth, and that there is nothing in his personality or background to justify his leadership role. In particular, Kiernan is highly critical of Arafat's past connections with the Ikhwan Muslimin (Muslim Brotherhood).

Kiernan's text also contains outright historical errors and distortions of fact. For example, he claims that an unnamed member of the Wafd party in Egypt, "disgusted with the secret corruption and graft,"[13] published an exposé at the end of the war of 1948 that assisted the Brotherhood in its struggle for power. In the same sentence, Kiernan also states that the Egyptian economy was on the verge of collapse. Actually, the book, published by Makram Ubayd, who had been thrown out of the Wafd leadership, was published in the middle of the war. The Black Book and its sequel were used by King Faruq, who detested the Wafd, as an excuse to dismiss the Wafdist government. Owing to the exigencies of the war, there was a severe inflationary spiral in Egypt, but the economy itself, based primarily on cotton and agricultural products which were in demand, was not on the verge of collapse. There was, however, a need for more equitable distribution of the wealth generated by the relative prosperity of the Egyptian economy. Kiernan also alleges that Queen Nazli was the real power behind the throne. On the contrary, it was public knowledge that Faruq violently disliked his mother, and subsequently disowned her.

Elsewhere, Kiernan notes that "the well-equipped Egyptian armies were repelled by the comparatively ill-equipped Israelis in 1948" (p. 129). It is well-known and documented that the Egyptian army used second-hand British discards because much of the equipment meant for the army was sold by the corrupt officer corps on the black market to the highest bidders. In regard to

---

[13]Thomas Kiernan, *Yasir Arafat*, London: ABACUS, Sphere, 1976, p. 128. In contrast, see: Alan Hart, *Arafat: Terrorist or Peacemaker?* London: Sidgwick & Jackson, 1984.

Nasser's regime, Kiernan alleges that its leaders immediately announced their intention to annihilate Israel. In fact, the Egyptian-Israeli borders from 1952 to 1954 were relatively quiet and it was the Israelis who frequently launched attacks across the borders. Kiernan's descriptions of the 1956 war and Arafat's involvement in it are equally distorted. Indeed, Kiernan's text contains so many factual errors regarding events which are well-documented in public archives that his account of Arafat and the PLO, subjects which are not so well-documented, must be held to severe scrutiny.

Kiernan's pro-Israeli bias becomes more pronounced as he draws closer to the present. At one point, he states that Israel planned to divert the Jordan River only after the Arabs "had refused to join in a joint water management plan with the Jewish state" (p. 140). Kiernan fails to mention the American Johnston plan, an attempt by the Eisenhower administration to alleviate the Palestinian refugee problem by settling the refugees on newly irrigated land provided by the Jordan diversion. The plan allotted Israel about 40 percent of the available water and, from the Arab perspective, seemed to imply their de facto recognition of Israel. The Arab nations ultimately rejected the plan. What Kiernan does not point out is that Israel, which was unhappy with its allotted share and opposed U.N. supervision of the plan, also rejected the proposal and responded by announcing a plan of its own. Kiernan's discussion of this period is based almost entirely on Israeli interpretations. While assuming the validity of Israeli actions, Kiernan criticizes the motivations of all Arab leaders. He speaks authoritatively on the activities of the Israeli intelligence services, noting that they "had not taken notice of Fatah until late 1964" (p. 204). He goes on to point out that by 1968 the Israelis "had a rather thorough knowledge of Fatah—its makeup, its leadership, and especially the locations of its staging bases in Jordan" (p. 217). Although, Kiernan does not document this information, it seems to parallel studies by noted Israeli specialists such as Harkabi.

Kiernan's sources become fewer and more obscure as he describes Arafat's emergence as a political leader. At this juncture, Kiernan's narrative is studded with hyperbole and value judgments. He describes the Fatah commandos as Arafat's "minions." He alleges that Fatah was paid "larger and larger amounts of money out of the treasuries of sheikhs who were rich beyond imagination" (p. 219). At this point, Kiernan has substituted gross generalizations for hard research or academic objectivity.

Kiernan's outrage peaks when he describes Arafat's 1974 visit to the United Nations. Kiernan's description of Arafat's U.N. speech is instructive not only for its lack of objectivity, but also as an example of how omission and distortion can be manipulated to give a desired impression:

> To Israel it was, of course, an outrage. To the majority of nations, however, many of them born of terrorism and guerrilla warfare, the Palestinian cause was a kindred one and Arafat a kind of spiritual brother. Indeed, the very man elected as president of the General Assembly during the session in which Arafat was to speak was himself a former Algerian terrorist.
>
> As Arafat stood before the General Assembly and accepted its welcoming ovation he was, in the eyes of many, a sympathetic figure. Dressed in his familiar soiled khaki windbreaker and checked kaffiyah, which hid his totally bald pate, and with a holster on his hip, he read his carefully prepared speech—the product of the combined efforts of his closest Fatah colleagues—in an alternating compound of stentorian and pleading Arabic. It was a speech of contrasts—truths and untruths, historical accuracies and inaccuracies, threats and mollifications—all symbolized by the image he used to conclude it: the gun and the olive branch.
>
> As a speech it told the world everything it could want to know about Palestinian aspirations. It told the world everything it could want to know about Yasir Arafat. At the same time, it told the world nothing about either (p. 220).

Kiernan's assumption is that Israel was perfectly justified in its moral outrage. As a Westerner and Zionist sympathizer, he adopts a superior position from which to judge the relative rights of one nationalism against another. Indeed, Kiernan dismisses most Third World nationalism as having been born out of terrorism. He totally ignores the terrorist activities of Zionism prior to and after the creation of Israel. He also ignores the fact that most Third World nations gained independence after protracted struggles against Western imperial powers.

Kiernan excoriates the long Algerian national struggle while failing to note that the Algerians were forced to fight against French determination to keep Algeria as part of their African empire. Kiernan evidently considers that Israel, conceived with the support of the Western imperial powers, was justified in whatever means it adopted to secure independence. However, for Kiernan, other nations that fought against the West were not so justified.

Kiernan then makes a series of disparaging remarks about Arafat's appearance. He describes Arafat's dress as dirty, an adjective often used in a demeaning context. By innuendo, Kiernan implies that Arafat wears the traditional *kaffiyah* not to symbolize Palestinian national dress, but rather to cover his baldness. Arafat, of course, does not dress to please the West, but to reflect his position as leader of a people involved in a stuggle to achieve national self-determination. The *kaffiyah* is symbolic of the Palestinian nation. The khaki fatigues, gun holster and beard indicate Arafat's role as an active participant in the struggle of his people for a homeland. The dress also sets him apart from the medal-bedecked military leaders and neatly tailored politicians.

Arafat, who seemingly can do no right, is criticized for reading a prepared speech written collectively by members of Fatah. Kiernan avoids having to analyze the causes of the conflict over Palestine by alleging that the distortions in the speech are too obvious to discuss. As with matters of dress and personal style, Arafat's public statements must reflect the consensus of the Palestine Liberation Organization. The PLO is an umbrella organization consisting of members representing a wide spectrum of political viewpoints. In addition, Arafat represents the national aspirations of Palestinians scattered throughout the world and, most important, those in the occupied territories of the West Bank and the Gaza Strip. It is indicative of his acumen as a politician that he has been able to hold these disparate groups together. At the same time, he has managed to maneuver among conflicting Arab nations while keeping the PLO from being subsumed by any single Arab government. Arafat's personal qualities have served him particularly well in light of the 1982 war and subsequent attempts by rebel Palestinian factions backed by Syria to split the movement.

Rather than engage in a full, meaningful discussion of the Arab-Israeli conflict, Kiernan categorically condemns the Palestinians and Arafat as terrorists. Accordingly, Kiernan believes that Arafat will remain the major Palestinian leader because "they have made a habit of fiction-as-fact" (p. 223).

Finally, Kiernan predicts that Arafat and the Palestinians will "doubtless endeavor to bring about another war. . . . But this time their ambitions will not be limited to an Arab-Israeli war." They are already looking beyond the frontiers of the Middle East (p. 223). In fact, Kiernan is forewarning the West of the dangers presented by the Palestinians. Having recognized these dangers, Kiernan urges that the West protect itself by destroying the menace by whatever means necessary. Exhortations such as these were used by Ariel Sharon and others to justify the Israeli invasion of Lebanon in 1982. Kiernan's work vilifies not only Arafat, but the entire Palestinian national cause. One of the pernicious effects of works such as Kiernan's is that they defame the Arab world, while never so much as paying lip service, let alone giving thoughtful, incisive comment, to the Palestinians or the Arab cause. The end result is that the reader is deluged with works which revile the Palestinians and the Arabs in general. The contemporary reader receives practically no input to balance this negative picture.

There are few works that present a positive picture of the Arab Muslim world. For example, there are practically no autobiographical works by leading Arab figures. For this reason the books by Mohamed Heikal and Anwar Sadat assume unusual importance. However, they do not indicate the variety or sophistication of Arab political views.

A professional journalist, Heikal writes in a light, almost chatty fashion. His memoirs include numerous personal vignettes which often throw humanizing, if not incisive, light on leaders who heretofore have seemed somewhat distant to the average Western reader. Like many journalists, Heikal has an eye for the "good story," the humorous and the dramatic. However, his works often do not appear in paperback; the higher cost and limited distribution of his books prevent them from reaching the general audience.

In *Sphinx and Commissar*, Heikal describes crucial events in Egyptian and Middle East history. As former editor of the influential *Al-Ahram* newspaper and a close confidant of the late President Nasser, Heikal is in an unusual position to reveal the motivations behind the tempestuous history of the Egyptian-Soviet detente, the planning for the 1973 war and the interpersonal rivalries of key Egyptian leaders.

Heikal frankly relates the details of Egyptian relations with the Soviet Union and is equally open about his respect for Nasser. He recounts in *Sphinx and Commissar* how Nasser had predicted that Egyptian-Soviet relations would pass from the early honeymoon phase to one of wariness and difficulty. Heikal's conclusion that the Arabs seem to be moving increasingly to the right and that the Soviets have lost a large measure of support in the region is coldly analytical. He is much more equivocal about Anwar Sadat, with whom he openly split in 1974. His recent biography, *Autumn of Fury: The Assassination of Sadat*, traces his disagreements with the late Egyptian leader.

Heikal makes no secret of his opposition to Israel. He writes from the Egyptian perspective. However, in contrast to many Israeli writers, he is almost curiously devoid of personal hostility toward the enemy. He avoids the virulent, emotional accusations against Israel which characterize so much written about Arabs by his Western and Israeli counterparts.

Similarly, Anwar Sadat's autobiography, *In Search of Identity*, is less a discussion of the Arab-Israeli conflict than it is an introspective account of Sadat's personal struggles for success. A self-styled visionary with deep religious convictions, Sadat describes his early nationalist politics, his imprisonment for terrorist activities and his almost accidental accession to power following Nasser's unexpected death in 1970.

He is much less expansive about his political career during Nasser's presidency. An ambitious but extremely cautious politician, Sadat obviously resented the long years spent in Nasser's shadow. He constantly disparages Nasser's achievements. Occasionally, Sadat is personally and politically hostile to Nasser. He also tends to aggrandize his own importance during Nasser's regime. In fact, Nasser tended to underestimate Sadat's abilities; for Nasser, Sadat remained the loyal, if plodding assistant. After Sadat's accession to the presidency, even U.S. intelligence agents in the field predicted his tenure in office would not exceed four months. In light of subsequent events, one must conclude that Sadat's political acumen far surpassed even Nasser's expectations.

Sadat emphasizes that the 1973 war and his 1977 visit to Jerusalem were the results of his own initiatives. He does not credit Israeli intelligence reports with providing an incentive for the Jerusalem trip. By contrast, Sidney Zion and Uri Dan in the "Untold Story of the Mideast Talks," published in *The New York Times,* have alleged that Israeli reports played a key role in Sadat's decisions regarding the peace initiative.[14] According to Sadat, he alone had decided Egypt desperately needed peace.

Having engineered the 1973 war, which Sadat considers a victory and for which he takes full credit, he then wanted to effect a lasting peace. When referring to the 1973 war, Sadat generally avoids using the term "the Ramadan war." The 1973 Arab-Israeli war occurred in October, which in that year happened to be the Muslim holy month of Ramadan, a time of fasting and spiritual renewal. Within the Islamic world some Mulsims refer to the 1973 war as the Ramadan war because it took place in that month. Hence Heikal entitled his book on the background to the war *The Road to Ramadan*, but in the text he refers to the October 1973 war. Similarly, Lieutenant General Saad el-Shazly, Egyptian Chief of Staff during the war, referred to the "October war." In the West the term Ramadan war was generally taken to be synony-

---

[14]Sidney Zion and Uri Dan, "Untold Story of the Mideast Talks," *The New York Times* (Sunday Magazine), January 21 and 28, 1979.

mous with *jihad* or holy war, as noted in el-Shazly's *The Crossing of the Suez*.

In contrast, Israelis almost universally use the term "Yom Kippur war," which implies not only that the war began on that Jewish holy day, but that they were the innocent victims of the attack. The usage tends to obfuscate the fact that the Egyptians were seeking to regain their own territory in the Sinai that had been occupied by the Israelis since the 1967 war. Writers and politicians who have sought a neutral position have generally preferred to avoid these value-laden terms and to refer to the war simply as the 1973 Arab-Israeli war.

Sadat also reaffirms the need for a Palestinian state; however, subsequent negotiations belie his commitment to this ideal. In justifying his Jerusalem visit, Sadat stresses Israel's existence as a political reality that should be recognized by the Arab nations. While hoping to remain in Nasser's position as leader of the Arab world, he believes that Egyptian interests should be primary. Recognizing the opposition his recognition of Israel would incite, Sadat argues that his approach is the correct one.

Like Heikal, Sadat does not dwell extensively on the Egyptian-Israeli antagonism. Sadat's account is in marked contrast to similar autobiographies by Israeli leaders. In Israeli accounts, the Arabs are very much the enemies who are held in both fear and contempt. That Israelis generally do not play a major role in Arab literature has been noted in studies by Abdulwahab Elmessiri, who has pointed to the marked difference between the Israeli preoccupation with the Arab enemy and the remarkable absence of Israelis as personalized enemies in most Arab writing.[15] Sadat underscores this difference by stressing that he has not intended to write an account of the Arab-Israeli conflict, but has aimed to describe his search for personal fulfillment. For Sadat, as for other Arab writers, the conflict with Israel was largely peripheral to the larger problems of social and economic development.

---

[15]Abdelwahab M. Elmessiri, ed., *A Lover From Palestine and Other Poems*, Washington, D.C.: Free Palestine Press, 1970.

However, even after the peace treaty between Egypt and Israel was concluded, popular publications in the West concentrated almost entirely upon Israeli and Western reactions. For example, *Flight into Egypt*, published by Pinnacle in paperback, explores the personal reaction of Amos Elon, a noted Israeli journalist and author. *The Year of the Dove*, issued by Bantam books and written by Eitan Haber, Zeev Schiff and Ehud Yaari, is another so-called instant history of the peace accords from an Israeli perspective. U.S. leaders, including former President Carter, have published accounts of the Camp David accords and have generally been highly sympathetic to Sadat.[16] Foreign Minister of Egypt Ismail Fahmy's *Negotiating for Peace in the Middle East*, which is sharply critical of Sadat, has only been published in expensive hardcover form by John Hopkins University Press. Similar books dealing with Arab responses—whether positive or negative—have not been published in paperback editions aimed for the general Western audience. Hence, in both volume and approach, popular biographical accounts tend to be heavily weighted toward Israeli interpretations.

---

[16]See the winter and summer 1983 issues of *American-Arab Affairs* for documentation of these accounts.

IV. "INSTANT" HISTORIES

Since the first Arab-Israeli war in 1948, the conflict has been a topic for instant histories. After every Arab-Israeli war, "pop" or "instant" histories that capitalize on public interest in the current crisis have appeared. These histories differ radically from scholarly studies in that the authors generally make little or no effort to provide full documentary evidence or references or to present a balanced, objective analysis. However, if the authors are well-known journalists, military officers or politicians, the reader often assumes that the books are based on complete first-hand knowledge. In the absence of full disclosure of evidence, misleading or erroneous conclusions can be sustained by the omission of relevant facts or by unsubstantiated assertions. Readers exposed only to these slanted narratives—to the exclusion of conflicting interpretations—are likely to form mistaken and highly subjective opinions as to the causes and nature of the conflict.

Instant histories focusing on the military aspects of the Arab-Israeli wars are particularly common. These range from the thoughtful *Diary of the Sinai Campaign* (on the 1956 war) by Moshe Dayan to the instant analysis of 1967 provided by Randolph and Winston S. Churchill in *The Six Day War*. The bulk of these military histories are from the Israeli perspective and vary considerably in quality. The personal accounts by Mordechai Gur and Saad el-Shazly exemplify the best of the popular histories. Lieutenant General Mordechai Gur's *The Battle for Jerusalem* is a fairly typical first-hand account by the commander of the paratroop forces that captured Jordanian-held Jerusalem in 1967. Although the work suffers by being a trifle long, it is generally a straightforward narrative of the military actions involved in the Israeli capture of Jerusalem. Lieutenant General Saad el-Shazly's *The Crossing of the Suez* is a comparable description of Egyptian military successes in 1973; however, while Gur's account appeared in an affordable paperback form, Shazly's report was only published in an expensive hardcover edition by American Mideast Research, a small firm with limited distribution capabilities. Neither of these relatively balanced narratives were as effective in dramatizing events and capturing the attention of the general audience as other more subjective and less accurate instant histories.

For example, the explosive titles *Strike Zion!* and *Zanek!* by William Stevenson immediately indicate their more propagandistic nature. Although advertised as complete histories of the 1967 war and the development of the Israeli air force, these two works are, in fact, highly impressionistic descriptions.

Stevenson, a former Royal Navy pilot, worked with the famous Sir William Stephenson, "Intrepid," during World War II and helped in undercover work to establish Israel. In spite of this close association with Israel, Stevenson is characterized in promotional accounts as a journalist who has spent considerable time in the Middle East. Leon Uris, author of *Exodus*, has praise for both of Stevenson's works. Calling *Zanek!* a "stirring document," Uris adds a postscript entitled "The Third Temple" to *Strike Zion!*. In this postscript, Uris reiterates Stevenson's sweeping glorification of Israeli achievements in the 1967 war and blames the Arabs for the conflict. Uris rhetorically wonders if the Arabs will see that "a cancer of hate and disease and hunger and ignorance blights their land. The Jews of Israel can and will bring light to the Arabs."[1] Uris, like other Zionists, insists that all Arabs are backward, disease-ridden and ignorant. From his perspective only the Western-educated, technically-advanced Israelis can bring the region into the modern world.

Both of Stevenson's books contain large pictorial sections featuring Israeli military leaders, the latest military equipment and "on the spot" news photographs taken in the heat of battle. Stevenson's books are clearly aimed for the popular audience. *Zanek!* appeared in paperback and hardcover; *Strike Zion!* was published as a paperback immediately following the 1967 war and was in its fourth printing within the year. *Zanek!*, the longer of the two, does

---

[1]William Stevenson, *Strike Zion!* New York: Bantam, 1967, p. 141.

not provide a chronological account of the history of the Israeli air force. It is an almost novelistic series of vignettes that focus on personalities and dramatic events. Stevenson lavishly praises the Israelis but fails to impart the sense of growth and achievement that a full, more balanced account might have done.

Ezer Weizman's *On Eagles' Wings* is one of the more successful literary works of this genre. It is both an intensely personal account and a history of the Israeli air force. Weizman vividly describes his participation in the Israeli air force from its early days as the Palestine Aviation Club to its evolution as a supersonic force. In the early chapters, Weizman, nephew to Chaim Weizmann, one of the founding fathers of Israel, succeeds in recreating the emotional struggle of the early Zionist pioneers. He also captures the excitement and intense involvement of the early Israeli pilots. Passionately committed to Zionism, Weizman is equally dedicated to promoting the Israeli air force as vital to the continued well-being of Israel.

He is "hawkish" regarding the need for Israel to be a "Middle East mini-power"[2] and does not mask his political disenchantment with many Labor party leaders. His conservative politics led to his involvement with Menachem Begin, under whom he served as a cabinet minister. Although Weizman eventually disagreed with Begin, he has made his continued political ambitions well-known.

In *On Eagles' Wings* Weizman traces Israeli involvement in the 1948, 1956, 1967 and 1973 wars. Although he places particular emphasis on the contributions and victories of the air force, Weizman also writes of both his personal defeats and glories. He shows deep regard for his fellow pilots and men under his command. He praises the valor of the Israeli pilots, and is highly critical of Arab military forces. However, Weizman very realistically predicts "that the Arabs would overcome their weakness and, at a later stage in the unfinished struggle against Israel, convert quantity to quality" (p. 122). For all of his commitment to the religious foundations of Zionism and his intensely combative spirit, Weizman is more

---

[2]Ezer Weizman, *On Eagles' Wings,* New York: Berkley, 1976, p. 283.

61

realistic in his appraisal of the conflict than many of his compatriots. His pragmatic approach goes far toward explaining his split with Begin and his support for the peace negotiations with Sadat.

Weizman is not reluctant to refer to the Palestinians by name, or to note their problems; however, he does not go so far as to accept responsibility for the refugees. He thoroughly condemns Arab leaders, particularly Nasser, for their hostility to Israel and manipulation of the Palestinian question. Likewise, he roundly berates King Hussein for his weakness and delays in dealing with the PLO. Using military parlance, Weizman refers to guerrillas rather than "terrorists," the usual Zionist term, but gives the Israeli military the full credit for shattering the guerrilla movement in Jordan.

> It's a total distortion of the facts to claim that it was Hussein who broke the guerillas' back. Nonsense! The Israeli army did it, with its finest combat units. Hussein completed the job in September 1970 out of selfish considerations and in fear for his throne (p. 249).

The intensity of the fighting between the Palestinians and the Jordanian forces in September 1970 indicated that the back of the PLO certainly had not been broken by the Israeli military. A former Middle East correspondent for *The Christian Science Monitor*, John Cooley, has provided a detailed history of the PLO in his book *Green March, Black September*.[3] Although weakened by the September fighting, the PLO subsequently expanded both its social welfare programs and its struggle for international recognition. During the 1982 invasion of Lebanon the Israelis reiterated their intention to destroy or to "break the back" of the PLO; the fighting strength of the PLO was again severely damaged, but the organization, its leadership and Palestinian determination to secure a homeland all survived.

Weizman is similarly critical of the failure of Israeli leaders to take more overt military action during the "war of attrition" begun in 1969. He also blasts military leaders for their failures in the 1973

---

[3]John K. Cooley, *Green March, Black September*, London: Frank Cass, 1973.

war. Weizman duly notes the improvement of the Arab forces and concomitant deterioration in Israeli commanders and intelligence services. By being so blunt, Weizman, the devoted Zionist, hopes to encourage Israel to take firmer stands against Arab opposition and to support more dynamic leadership. Weizman expanded on these themes in *The Battle for Peace*, in which he gives his personal interpretations of the relationships among Sadat, Carter and Begin during the Camp David meetings.

While *On Eagles Wings* and other military histories often read like novels, books on Israeli intelligence exploits read like action-packed adventure stories. Belief in the invincibility of the Israeli secret services has been widespread, not only in the West, but within much of the Arab world as well. Writers and former intelligence agents have often ranked the Israeli service among the world's best.

The Israelis have sought to popularize the belief in the supremacy of their secret services and to discredit or belittle Arab intelligence work. A number of Israeli agents and intelligence directors have written popular books. After the 1973 war, which incited considerable recriminations within Israel, a number of books appeared that extolled the flamboyant successes of the Israeli intelligence agencies. Intended for the Israeli public and its Western allies, these works sought to dispel the doubts about Israeli superiority that had been raised by the initially successful Egyptian attack across the Suez Canal.

These accounts laud the courage, determination and ingenuity of Israeli secret agents, while portraying the Arab services as inept, crude and barbaric. The "good guy" Israelis, their right backed up by might, almost always triumph over the "bad guy" Arabs. The reader concludes that the Israeli victories against the Arabs are, in fact, triumphs for the Western world. For example, *The Mossad* by Dennis Eisenberg, Uri Dan and Eli Landau purports to be a full history of the Israeli intelligence service. These writers have collaborated on other works and Uri Dan is reputed to have close ties with the Israeli intelligence community. The opening chapters of the book detail the development of the Shai, the intelligence branch of the Hagana; the Shin Beth, an internal security agency; and Aman, the Israeli military intelligence agency. The Mossad was assigned the tasks of gathering international intelligence information, implementing "special jobs" and carrying out "unusual assignments." The latter have varied from kidnapping Adolf Eichmann, to planting well-placed agents within the Arab nations, to assassinating leaders of various Palestinian organizations. The authors detail the successes of the Mossad, devoting each chapter to a single Israeli espionage success, such as the theft of a MIG and the passing on of military information to U.S. intelligence services.[4]

The Mossad is a dramatic and highly emotive study of the personalities and exploits of this particular branch of the Israeli secret services. It is not a balanced, chronological history on a level with Richard Deacon's study, *Israeli Secret Service*, although both books are overwhelmingly laudatory of Israeli intelligence successes. However, the cover of *The Mossad* misleadingly promotes the book as an academic, that is to say, objective, well-researched account.

The selective use and slanted presentation of material is also evident in books by former Israeli intelligence officers. In *The House on Garibaldi Street*, Isser Harel, former chief of Israel's secret service, relates the events behind the kidnapping of Adolf Eichmann in Argentina. Harel reconstructs the discovery of Eichmann's hiding place and the decision to abduct him and reproduces the alleged conversations of the agents responsible for the assignment. This technique makes the narrative flow smoothly while imparting an air of immediacy to the prose. As Harel intends, the reader is quickly caught up in the adventure.

Harel never discusses the moral and legal implications of Israel's abduction of Eichmann. The Argentine government loudly pro-

---

[4]Such exchanges of information are fairly commonplace. The United States has also occasionally paid for Israeli information. At one point these funds were to be channeled to Israeli intelligence operations in Africa, where Israel acted as a conduit for U.S. interests. *Newsweek*, September 3, 1979.

tested this public infringement of their national sovereignty by a foreign government. That the state of Israel did not attempt to go through the internationally recognized channels regarding extradition raised many legal and diplomatic questions. The kidnapping of an individual by a government also set a questionable precedent. The issue was not whether Eichmann should have been tried as a Nazi war criminal, but rather the manner in which the Israelis effected his capture. Israel subsequently publicly tried Eichmann and found him guilty. Although Israel does not have capital punishment, an exception was made in the Eichmann case and he was ultimately executed for his crimes.

Harel argues that Israel has the right to bring any Nazi criminal to trial. In the face of this special right, international law and the rights of other nations and individuals can, in Harel's opinion, be legitimately breached. *The House on Garibaldi Street* is predicated upon this assumption, which the casual reader tends to accept without question. Harel concludes that news of Eichmann's capture imbued "all decent people with a feeling of respect; and it carried with it a clear warning to the murderers of the Jewish people. . . ."[5]

Based on the same assumptions regarding the special rights of Israel, *Operation Uranium Ship* is the story of the theft and delivery of uranium cargo for use in an Israeli nuclear reactor. As the book cover loudly proclaims, it is "the true, inside story of an exploit that makes any fiction look tame." In *Operation Uranium Ship*, Eisenberg and Landau collaborated with Menahem Portugali, a pseudonym for two Israeli writers. In order to heighten the dramatic impact, the authors, who had access to the agents involved, reconstruct the dialogue so that the book reads like a thriller.

The uranium was delivered to Israel in 1968. Following the 1967 Arab-Israeli war the French government, led by Charles de Gaulle, who had previously announced France would cease sending military equipment to whatever nation initiated hostilities, placed an

---

[5]Isser Harel, *The House on Garibaldi Street*, New York: Viking, 1975; Bantam, 1976, p. 319.

embargo on all military shipments to Israel. The embargo included uraninum, even though the French had been assisting the Israelis in building an atomic reactor. To compensate for this loss, the Israeli secret service stole 200 tons of uranium from a ship bound from West Germany to Genoa, Italy. The uranium had been under the supervision of Euratom, the European Communities' nuclear regulatory agency; the Israeli operation involved undercover work in Europe, the hijacking and diversion of the ship and the theft of the uranium itself. The matter was highly embarrassing to the European Economic Community, which suspected Israel, but in the absence of proof the matter was quietly ignored. The theft of the uranium was not made public until 1977 at an anti-nuclear conference in Austria. In the face of growing public hostility to the proliferation of nuclear weapons, Israel then decided to "leak" its nuclear capability and to attempt to justify its actions. The book constantly emphasizes that Israel's theft was both right and desirable. The authors do not deal with the moral implications of the theft, or with Israel's arrogant disregard for the European organizations responsible for the uranium. More important, the global implications of the proliferation of nuclear weapons are totally ignored. Nor does the account even mention that although many Arab nations, including Iraq, have signed the Nuclear Non-Proliferation Treaty, Israel not only has refused to do so, but has rejected international inspection of its Dimona reactor. The potential of nuclear confrontation in the Middle East made possible by Israel's nuclear capability is disregarded. In both *Operation Uranium Ship* and *The House on Garibaldi Street* the fast-moving, glamorized narratives are calculated to obscure the important moral issues raised by Israeli actions.

The success of Israeli agents in infiltrating Arab nations has been another favorite subject for popular histories. A first-hand account, *The Champagne Spy*, traces the operations in Egypt of Wolfgang Lotz. His blond Nordic features made a perfect cover for Lotz, who posed as a rich breeder of thoroughbred horses. With limitless funds provided by the Mossad, Lotz entertained ranking Egyptian army officers in grand style. His hospitality and opulent gifts earned him an entree into Egyptian society. Using his wealth and assuming an anti-Semitic attitude as a cover, Lotz gathered vital information on German scientists working in Egypt, troop movements and other top secret material. Lotz was so successful that the Mossad relaxed internal rules to accept his marriage to a German woman, Waltrud, who was subsequently also recruited into the service of Israeli intelligence.

Lotz's story is a glowing rendition of luxurious living and high adventure. After the interception of his wireless messages, Lotz and his wife were arrested. Lotz avers that agents from an unnamed power (possibly the Soviet Union) tracked down the information and passed it on to the Egyptians. Lotz, his wife and several Egyptians were tried and sentenced to prison terms. After their release in 1968, Lotz and his wife went to Israel, where Waltrud died. Lotz then moved to the United States, married an Israeli, and later moved to Germany, where he talked of returning to Egypt. His narrative reveals a curious love-hate relationship with the Egyptians. Lotz, an opportunist with ill-defined political convictions, plainly liked living in Egypt and enjoyed the opulent lifestyle his undercover activities permitted.

These books provide an instructive look into how intelligence services, including Israel's, make use of outside agencies, blinds and foreign nationals. Bribes, ruses, wiretapping and misuse of uniforms, titles and insignias are commonplace. Acclaim for the Israeli secret service peaked after the raid on Entebbe airport in Uganda in July 1976, when two Palestinians from the Popular Front for the Liberation of Palestine (PFLP) and two Germans hijacked an Air France plane en route from Tel Aviv to Paris via Athens. The plane was taken to the Entebbe airport, where it was met by Ugandan troops under Idi Amin. Although a number of passengers were subsequently released, negotiations dragged on and the Israelis decided to take matters into their own hands by sending troops to gain the release of the passengers. Entebbe became a "media event" featured on Western television, radio and in the press. William Stevenson's *90 Minutes at Entebbe* typifies the coverage of this incident. Stevenson, whose earlier books have been discussed, credits Uri Dan, an author of other pro-Israeli accounts, with providing much of the background information for the Entebbe book. In the manner of many instant histories, Stevenson's narrative is relatively short. The bulk of the book is filled with action photographs and an extended text of the United Nations debate on the raid. It also includes a transcript of the rather bizarre telephone conversations that took place between Colonel Baruch Bar-Lev and Idi Amin, who knew a number of the commanders personally because of his military training in Israel. These appendixes account for a third of the total text.

Stevenson describes guerrilla warfare as seeking to "destroy the decencies." Israel's decision to embark on the raid, or Operation Thunderbolt, is described as "a unique test of democracy under siege."[6] Stevenson condemns all terrorists. Carlos, referred to as the Jackal, is often mentioned, as is Wadi Haddad, a key strategist for the Marxian Popular Front for the Liberation of Palestine (PFLP), who is described as an arch-terrorist with a string of mistresses (pp. 3, 46, 53, 55).

Stevenson reiterates that Israel is responsible for all Jews wherever they are. Because the hostages at Entebbe were Jewish, Israel had, therefore, the right to act in their defense. In his introduction Stevenson contends that because "the barter of the innocent for the criminal is still not regarded as moral" by Israel, it has the right to take any action against such crimes. This is essentially the same premise used to justify the Eichmann kidnapping and the uranium theft. Stevenson's *90 Minutes at Entebbe* and most Western media accounts obscured several vital aspects of the conflict between the Israelis and the Palestinians. These accounts present a highly simplistic picture of the conflict and ignore the diverse political viewpoints contained within the PLO. The division over ideologies and tactics between the PFLP and Fatah, the largest single group within the PLO, is not noted. Similarly, there is no mention that Arafat and the PLO had publicly opposed such

---

[6]William Stevenson with material from Uri Dan, *90 Minutes at Entebbe*, New York: Bantam, 1976, p. 55.

hijackings. Israel in particular sought to portray and condemn all Palestinian groups as identical. Nor do these accounts grapple with the basic question as to why some Palestinians have engaged in terrorism. Terrorism is not the first strategy that disenfranchised people adopt. Indeed, those Palestinian political groups that adopted terrorism did so as a "politics of desperation" after sustained efforts to gain international recognition of their right to self-determination had failed.

The Stevenson account not only reveals the international scope of Israeli intelligence activities, but also underscores the extent to which some secret services work in collusion with one another. For example, early in 1976 several Palestinians were apprehended trying to shoot down an El Al airplane with Soviet missiles as it landed at Nairobi airport. Jomo Kenyatta arranged for them to be interrogated secretly by Israeli agents. There was also close cooperation between Israelis and Kenyans during Operation Thunderbolt. Stevenson notes that British intelligence assisted in the raid. Lebanese security reports are also alluded to by Stevenson, who notes that when the Israelis had attempted to assassinate the Palestinian Wadi Haddad, the man responsible for launching the rocket attack on Haddad's Beirut apartment held an Iranian passport. That agent subsequently made his way to West Germany; however, Stevenson leaves it to the reader's imagination to recognize the actual nationality of the agent. There was also cooperation by both U.S. and Iranian secret services. Stevenson adds that Israeli agents had free access to the hostages released from Uganda after they arrived in Paris.

Subsequent books have completely exonerated Israel from all guilt in its assassinations of Palestinian leaders and suspected terrorists. In fact, *The Hit Team* by David B. Tinnin with Dag Christensen, parts of which originally appeared in *Playboy*, and *Vengeance* by George Jonas actually glorify the Israeli "hit teams" that were responsible for the killing of Palestinian leaders in Europe.[7]

---

[7]David B. Tinnin with Dag Christensen, *The Hit Team*, New York: Dell, 1976; George Jonas, *Vengeance*, New York: Simon and Schuster, 1984.

In *The Hit Team* Tinnin argues that his book seeks to balance the record regarding news accounts of the assassinations, which included the murder of at least one innocent man. On the same pattern as *The House on Garibaldi Street*, *Vengeance* is written in the present tense with novelistic recreations of conversations and actions of the so-called Israeli "counter-terrorist team." In both these books, Palestinian use of terrorism is condemned while Israeli use of violence and assassination is both justified and condoned.

By contrast, the Arabs and the Arab intelligence services in particular are largely isolated from such friendly espionage exchanges and, in popular writing, are roundly condemned. For example, Yaacov Caroz's *The Arab Secret Services*, published in 1978, is a vitriolic, blanket condemnation of Arabs. Deputy Chief of the Mossad under Isser Harel, Caroz has expert knowledge of the espionage war within the Middle East. However, for an academic work the book contains a number of peculiarities. There is no table of contents and only newspapers are cited as references. As an espionage agent, Caroz presumably employs sources that he is not at liberty to reveal; however, he also enjoins his readers to skip over the beginning chapters devoted to the theories and motivations for espionage activities. In other words, the reader is encouraged to proceed directly to the action chapters and leave the ideological motivations for espionage to the experts.

Although Caroz announces his intention to provide a history of the Arab secret services, he actually presents a long list of their alleged barbarities and failures. The Egyptian secret services are extensively described, while the Iraqi agency is singled out in a particularly critical chapter. In the chapter "From Pharaoh to Nasser" Caroz refers to Egypt as an "intelligence state." Actually, the chapter does not trace Egyptian espionage activities back to ancient times, but opens with a "swarthy man"[8] on an airplane.

---

[8] Yaacov Caroz, *The Arab Secret Services*, London: Corgi, Transworld Publishers, 1978, p. 20.

In popular literature "swarthy" is generally a tag word used to indicate an Arab.

Caroz discusses attempts to overthrow Nasser's regime and his relationship with the CIA. He mentions the various successes in intelligence work that the Israelis have achieved in Egypt, several of which have already been described. He notes that the Egyptians have maintained that the spies they have caught had been under surveillance for several years. Allowing that the Egyptians might have kept some agents under surveillance for three years, Caroz doubts that the Egyptians would actually keep most agents under surveillance for such an extended period, as it is "unlikely that superstition or hallowed tradition obliges Egyptian Intelligence to specify a period of three years" (p. 132).

By deprecating the Egyptians, Caroz seeks to undercut the successes that they have had in ferreting out Israeli agents. Caroz does not mention the ethical ramifications of Israeli espionage activities in Egypt; in particular, he totally ignores the famous Lavon affair. In 1954 Israeli intelligence, apparently without the knowledge of Pinchas Lavon, the defense minister, instigated a scheme to explode bombs at United States offices in Cairo. These explosions would demonstrate anti-Western feelings within Egypt and were aimed at spoiling U.S. and British relations with Egypt. The Lavon affair was a classic example of *agent provocateur* tactics. The prompt Egyptian discovery of the plot caused an upheaval in the Israeli government and ruling circles that lasted for years.

The difficulties involved in direct intervention in Arab affairs, however, did not deter sections of the Israeli leadership from continuing to try to effect a change in the Nasser regime. As the Israelis kept a close eye on all former Nazis, they used their presence in Egypt to discredit Nasser's regime as neo-fascist. Caroz makes heavy use of irony when describing Nazi scientists in Egypt, but has only praise for Israeli espionage successes against Arab states, NATO and the United Nations, which he severely censures.

71

While highly critical of the Egyptians, Caroz is most caustic when discussing Syrian and Iraqi intelligence agencies led by the Baath party, which Caroz defines as "a Secret Superservice" (p. 387). The Iraqi Baath is accused of liquidating its victims and of having "recklessly persecuted" its enemies. Caroz excoriates the Iraqis for engaging in little or no "positive intelligence work" while concentrating only on Iran and Israel (p. 394). He fails to note that Iran and Israel have been Iraq's major enemies for the past several decades. The Syrian branch of the Baath party has tended to concentrate on internal security problems, but, in Caroz's words, "still found time to act against Israel" (p. 295).

Caroz is highly sympathetic to the Iranian regime under the Shah. In fact, the Shah maintained relatively open relations with Israel. Israeli agents helped, with CIA assistance, to train agents of SAVAK, the Shah's infamous secret service. Caroz rebukes the Iraqi regime for allowing members of the Iranian underground opposed to the Shah to be trained in Iraq.

Not surprisingly, Caroz is vehemently critical of the Palestinians. However, he does not deal directly with the PLO except insofar as its activities relate to the Lebanese civil war, which is discussed at length. Omitting specific details on Israeli intelligence activities in Lebanon, Caroz does mention that Beirut served as the center for intelligence operations.

Caroz also acknowledges the cooperation among Israeli, British and U.S. intelligence agencies. From his point of view this mutual assistance grew out of the common interests held by the democratic nations of the West and from their desire to stem the tide of Soviet and Arab expansion. Although he does not cite sources, Caroz alludes to Israeli knowledge of domestic affairs within Palestinian organizations, Jordan and Lebanon. He implies that elements within Jordan and Lebanon have worked with Israel; the open cooperation of the Lebanese Kataeb or Phalange, as it is still often called, and the Israelis during and after the 1982 war substantiate these claims (pp. 194, 293).

After the 1973 war the Israeli intelligence services were severely criticized for failing to predict the Egyptian invasion across the Suez. Caroz rationalizes these failures:

72

> *A miracle did in fact occur . . . Israeli intelligence was temporarily struck blind, despite the flood of information and the clear indications available to it. . . . The Israeli Intelligence evaluation resulted from a stale approach rather than from cold analysis of the facts* (p. 231).

Published in 1978, *The Arab Secret Services* stresses the failures of Arab intelligence services while reaffirming the almost total infallibility of the Israeli services. In a final denunciation, Caroz emphasizes that in 1967 and 1973 the vital information on the Israeli military was provided to the Arabs by the Soviet Union. He concludes that the Arab governments spend proportionately more of their budgets on intelligence; however, he does not provide specific data regarding either Arab or Israeli expenditures for intelligence work. Intelligence expenditures are not generally listed in a separate category in national budgets, but are subsumed under foreign and military expenses. Consequently, any estimates of how much a nation expends on intelligence activities is highly speculative at best. Nowhere does Caroz discuss the organization, leadership or internal structures of the Arab intelligence agencies. Although he admits that all nations engage in espionage activities, Caroz seeks to demonstrate that the Arab secret services act outside the so-called "rules." More balanced studies by Philip Agee, Miles Copeland and Andrew Tully amply demonstrate that all secret services act upon motivations and employ methods which are virtually identical.[9] These studies detail various intelligence service activities, in particular CIA involvement in planting spies and eavesdropping, committing assassinations and inciting wars. Israeli intelligence services have been responsible not only for the aforementioned kidnapping, planting of bombs and theft of uranium but for the assassination of numerous Palestinians around the world.

Following the election of Menachem Begin as prime minister there was also a popular reassessment of Israeli history. *Terror*

---

[9]Philip Agee, *Inside the Company: CIA Diary*, London: Penguin, 1975; Miles Copeland, *The Real Spy World*, London: Sphere, 1974 and 1978; Andrew Tully, *The Super Spies*, New York: Pocket Books, 1970.

out of Zion: The Shock Troops of Israeli Independence by J. Bowyer Bell is just one example of this revisionism. These works emphasize the role of the Irgun and the Stern in the establishment of Israel. They also tend to be highly critical of the history presented by Labor Party leaders; hence they offer a different, but no less glorified, history of Israel to that given in the autobiographies of Meir, Dayan or Eban. Bell's account is laudatory of the Irgun and negative regarding the Palestinian Arabs. He recounts the hardline Zionist version of Israel's right to exist. In summary he concludes:

> *For this small state, this remnant of their dream, this special land redeemed from history, for this they called for terror out of Zion and not in vain.*[10]

The two themes of the historic validity of Zionism and the romanticized interpretation of the Zionist underground are interwoven throughout these revisionist histories.

The overwhelming majority of these works focus on events that portray the Israelis in the best possible light. Even a brief perusal demonstrates that they generally emphasize Israeli military and intelligence successes. They are based on the assumption that Zionism is a positive nationalist force—a force that should be supported by the Western world. In these popular histories the negative or less attractive aspects of Israeli history are ignored or minimized. Because the Western public has little or no background in the history of the Middle East, these highly slanted renditions are generally accepted as presenting the objective facts. Conversely, there are very few popular histories that portray the Arab world in favorable or even objective terms. Translation difficulties have contributed to this disparity. Then, too, except for Anwar Sadat and a few others, most Arab leaders have not taken advantage of the vehicle of autobiographies or memoirs to present their viewpoints to the Western audience. Nor have most Western

---

[10]J. Bowyer Bell, *Terror Out of Zion: The Shock Troops of Israeli Independence*, New York: Avon Discus, 1977, p. 443.

authors of instant histories sought either to present the Middle East or the Arab-Israeli conflict from the Arab perspective or from a neutral stance. In particular, the case for Palestinian self-determination and the evolution of their conflict with Israel has not been properly explored and explained in popular histories. Indeed, a number of these "histories" have depicted the Arab world and the Palestinians in entirely negative terms. Hence the picture of the Middle East corresponds directly to that drawn in popular biographies and, as will be demonstrated in the following chapters, in contemporary fiction.

V. NOVELS: ADVENTURE, ROMANCE AND INTERNATIONAL FINANCE

Middle Eastern themes figure prominently in the plots of adventure stories, romances and tales of international financial crises. In adventure novels Israeli heros are pitted against Arab villains. As in old style westerns, confrontations between the forces of good and evil are the staple of the genre.

In *Israeli Commandos* by Andrew Sugar the plot revolves around an Israeli hero who triumphs over enormous odds. The Israelis are all noble and courageous, the Arabs cowardly and barbaric. Part of an extended paperback series, *Israeli Commandos* is aimed at the popular audience that demands plots full of fast action. There is an act of violence or a sexual encounter every two or three pages. Similarly, *The Moroccan* by C.A. Haddad is advertised as featuring "Israel's sexiest superspy."[1]

The Last Temptation by Joseph Viertel is a panegyric to the creation of Israel. Although far less successful, it is strikingly similar in tone to *Exodus*. Full of local color, the book extols Israel as a Western outpost in a sea of turmoil and depicts the Arabs as the outside enemies. In a more contemporary vein, *The Jerusalem Conspiracy* by David Allen Riis centers on beautiful female agents and brave Israelis who struggle against terrorism. The book's cover shows an Arab terrorist, a belly dancer and an Israeli flag.[2]

In a variation of the "good guy versus bad guy" plots, *The Eichmann Syndrome* and *The Goering Testament* revolve around Israelis tracking down former or neo-Nazis. In addition to Israeli

---

[1]C.A. Haddad, *The Moroccan*, New York: Harper and Row, 1975; Bantam, 1978; Andrew Sugar, *Israeli Commandos*, New York: Manor Books, 1975.

[2]Joseph Viertel, *The Last Temptation*, New York: Simon & Schuster, 1955; Pocket Books, 1956; David Allen Riis, *The Jerusalem Conspiracy*, New York: Dell/Bryans Books, 1979.

heroes who emerge victorious against the forces of anti-Semitism and fascism, these novels are almost always anti-Arab in tone. Given Uri Dan's other writing credits, it is not surprising that in *The Eichmann Syndrome* he characterizes the 1948, 1956, 1967 and 1973 wars as preventing "another holocaust."[3] George Markstein in *The Goering Testament* stretches historical analysis by comparing the Balfour Declaration to the Declaration of Independence. Markstein's protagonist, a British journalist, is saved from the neo-Nazis by the Israeli Mossad. In these novels Israel is portrayed as the courageous underdog. The authors do not mention, as former Israeli Prime Minister Menachem Begin has, that, in particular, the 1956, 1967 and 1982 wars were "wars of choice" for Israel. Contrary to commonly held Western belief, Israel was not forced into these conflicts by the Arab nations, but elected to initiate hostilities in order to secure precise political and military goals.

Although the plots of these books revolve around Israelis, there are also numerous adventure novels in which the anti-Arab tone and impact are predominant. For example, in *The Sheik* by Maggie David there are oil-rich Arabs, Muslim fanatics and women plotting from behind harem walls. The richest man in the world, Abdullah, is depicted as selfish, superficial and irresistible to women. The author manipulates words so that even positive characteristics of the Arab world become somehow obscene. For example, Arabs are described as being protected by the "all-encompassing crotch of Arab kinship."[4] Anti-Arab one-liners such as this are scattered throughout many popular novels.

Even novels in which the Middle East is not crucial to plot development frequently contain anti-Arab stereotypes. For example, the novels by the best-selling author Trevanian often contain racist stereotypes. In *Shibumi*, which was a best-seller and Book-of-the-Month Club selection, Arabs are described as rug mer-

---

[3]Uri Dan with Edward Radley, *The Eichmann Syndrome*, New York: Leisure Books, 1977, p. 32.

[4]Maggie Smith, *The Sheik*, New York: Fawcett Crest, 1977, p. 12.

chants, as lascivious and as not suited for clothes requiring "posture and discipline."[5] In addition to belittling the traditional Arab robes and head garb well-suited to the climatic conditions of the Middle East, Trevanian spuriously slurs an entire multinational ethnic group, implying that rejection of Western dress reflects a character defect.

Trevanian also alludes to the seemingly higher than average libidinous drives among Arabs and to their involvement in commerce. While many Arabs are engaged in commercial pursuits, many more are peasants or in service industries such as teaching or medicine. Referring to Arabs solely as "rug merchants" implies a class structure that in no way reflects the reality of the economies in Arab nations. It also calls to mind the image of the greedy Arab merchant in *Exodus*.

Similarly, there is a marked sexual component in many of these narratives. The tendency is to attribute greater voluptuousness to the women of the out-group and greater libidinous drive to the men. The unknown, exotic or mysterious is portrayed as having an excessive sexuality. Hence in much Western literature Arab women are described as dark temptresses, while Arab men are presented as lusting after fair-haired maidens. The symbolic use of the dark versus light metaphor is clear. The use of black (depicting evil) juxtaposed with the white (depicting good) images reflects similar treatment of Blacks and Jews in Western culture. At one juncture in Western history such treatment of Blacks and Jews was fairly commonplace; however, with growing awareness of the prejudicial effects of such distorted and false stereotypes, neither group is popularly described in such terms in the contemporary era. However, such pernicious sexual stereotypes are still frequently applied with regard to Arabs. Attributing overweening sexuality and financial cupidity to an entire ethnic, racial or religious group has long been common in racist stereotyping.

Jews, Blacks and many others have traditionally suffered from identical misrepresentations. Through protracted struggle and

---

[5]Trevanian, *Shibumi*, New York: Random House, 1979; Ballantine, 1980, p. 5.

consciousness raising, most of these groups fortunately have succeeded in both refuting and checking the proliferation of such stereotypes. However, the racial stereotypes that have become unacceptable when applied to other groups are still commonly used with regard to Arabs. In some measure these anti-Arab stereotypes are perpetuated in popular fiction—and other media forms—because they are easy to use. A novelist knows that the Western audience will not only recognize, but accept the Arab stereotype. Hence the novelist's difficult task of character and plot development is minimized. Similarly, writers, particularly of pulp novels, use sex and violence as devices to propel the plot or to speed up the action.

James R. Baerg of CBS-TV's Program Practices Department has commented on similar stereotyping of Arabs in the electronic media. While noting that much of this stereotyping takes the form of "one-line" jokes, he also emphasizes that Western audiences have readily accepted these stereotypes.[6] Likewise the authors of *The Sheik, Shibumi* and many other novels include gratuitous anti-Arab stereotypes because they are convenient. These exaggerated and highly distorted versions of Arabs, Muslims and the Middle East have generally been accepted as legitimate by the overwhelming majority of readers.

Jordan Patrol by the Israeli writer Igal Lev is among the more thoughtful of the adventure novels. Although promoted like a Hollywood production, this work is far more sophisticated than the books discussed previously. The paperback cover of *Jordan Patrol*, featuring a scantily clad woman leaning seductively against a uniformed man, is highly reminiscent of covers for 1940s mysteries. Originally published in Hebrew, *Jordan Patrol* is a fictionalized firsthand account of the 1967 war. A former member of Zahal, Lev participated in Israeli raids into Jordan and Egypt. He writes about "reprisal raids" and "Israeli freedom fighters" from a personal perspective. The narrative perceptively describes the

---

[6]James R. Baerg, "Television Programming Practice," *The American Media and the Arabs*, pp. 45-48.

moral dilemmas of soldiers, men who are torn between love of their families and the constant reality of violence and death. The Israelis in the novel talk extensively about the Arab outsiders in the dichotomous "we-they" idiom typical of Israeli writings. The outsiders, the Arabs and Palestinians (never mentioned by name), are treated as hostile, usually faceless, enemies. In contrast, the Israelis as a group are portrayed as a peace-loving people who have been forced into war, while individual Israelis are particularized into believable characters.

In Lev's narrative the Palestinians in 1967 are "the refugees" or "silent columns of human beings"[7] fleeing because their irresponsible leaders have told them that they will be killed if they remain. In addition to the refusal of Israelis to face the reality of Palestinian existence, there is a tendency to blame the existence of the refugees on Arab leaders rather than on fear, Israeli actions or wartime exigencies. In fact, many of the refugees from the 1967 war had lived in camps in the West Bank, which was controlled by Jordan previous to 1967 but seized by Israel during the conflict. In the course of the war, many Palestinians fled the West Bank refugee camps to seek safety on the East Bank of the Jordan River. The majority of these people have never been permitted to return. In the novel the Israelis view the Arabs as the collective enemy and accept the view that Jerusalem was meant to be the heart of the Zionist state. Many, if not most, Israelis unquestioningly accept that the West Bank is an integral part of Israel.

Whereas the Israeli heroes are personalized, the Arab villages, domestic animals and people seem to exist only as props. Arab villages are described as primitive; Arab treatment of women is characterized as thoughtless and, at worst, cruel and sadistic. In *Exodus* Leon Uris described the treatment of Arab women in almost identical terms, distorting reality for propaganda purposes. In a particularly revealing scene in *Jordan Patrol*, the Israelis search the house of a poor Arab (again, never Palestinian) sheikh

---

[7]Igal Lev, *Jordan Patrol*, New York: Modern Literary Editions, trans. by Stanley A. Broza, 1970, p. 95.

and his family. In the cellar, during an exchange of machine-gun fire, the patrol kills a "Jordanian soldier, a young boy, perhaps the sheikh's eldest son" (p. 139). For the first time, the war becomes personalized for Lev, who writes that he suddenly realized

> . . . that a fighter should never see the face of the enemy . . . the same instant you take the insanity out of war, you transform it into something too realistic and cold. The death we have witnessed depressed us all.
> We demolished the house (p. 140).

Lev permits the reader a fleeting moment of pity for the Arab enemy and then counterattacks with the brutal reality—"We demolished the house." As if to compensate for the momentary sympathy for the enemy, Lev immediately shifts the focus to an Israeli soldier who remembers the 1956 Israeli attack on the Gaza Strip. He describes the Arabs as groveling cowards who only attacked after their enemies had turned their backs. In summary, the soldier concludes,

> I swore that I would never misjudge these Arabs again. . . .
> So Yankele did not speak about how sick it made him. He spoke only about the duty that was necessary (p. 142).

This passage underscores the fear that if the Israelis were to respond to their suffering, the Arab enemies would take advantage of the situation. To survive, the Israelis must be strong and vigilant, brutal, even rejecting of their own value system to survive. The deeper implication, which is emphasized in scenes throughout the book, is that the Israeli value system is based on honor and respect for life, but that the Arabs respect neither women nor children, and will stab a man in the back if given the slightest opportunity. In fact, Arab society consists of a complex interdependency of extended families. It places the highest value on the sanctity of the family, including women and children. The loyalty of individual Arabs to family and friends has been emphasized by innumerable observers. Writers as diverse as T.E. Lawrence (Lawrence of Arabia), Harry St. John Philby and Wilfred Thesiger, in addition to contemporary academics such as Morroe Berger and Louise Sweet, have all described loyalty, honor and familial respect as major components of Arab life.

This is not to say that the largely peasant society of Palestine, or any other peasant society for that matter, did not contain rival factions within it. Most peasant societies suffer from scarcity of land, goods and capital; consequently there is often keen competition for resources. Then too, as the well-known anthropologist Eric Wolf in *Peasant Wars of the 20th Century* and others have demonstrated, peasants are generally dominated by the wealthy landowning class, which constantly attempts to perpetuate its privileged position.[8] Within Palestine prior to the establishment of Israel in 1948, the peasantry had struggled not only against feudal landowners, but against domination by both the British and the Zionists. Indeed, the 1936 general strike and ensuing revolt that continued until 1939 was in some measure a Palestinian peasant rebellion. In the face of overwhelming British military superiority, opposition from the Zionists, and the failure of the large landowners to support it, the movement was ultimately crushed. However, the revolt clearly demonstrated the determination of the Palestinians to retain their land and their loyalty to the indigenous culture and society.

Later in *Jordan Patrol*, Lev describes the patrol engaging a group of Jordanian soldiers, who fight bravely. However, these Jordanians remain faceless; they are not individualized and lack reality. With victory, the Israelis engage in a joyous celebration, but the patrol continues to occupy the West Bank. During a subsequent reconnaissance mission, one member of the patrol is killed. The novel ends on the ironic note of soldiers mourning for their dead comrade at the same time that the nation celebrates its grand victory. The soldiers speak with bitterness about war, yet it is clear that the war will continue and that they will continue to fight.

---

[8]Eric Robert Wolf, *Peasant Wars of the 20th Century*, New York: Harper and Row, 1969.

Jordan Patrol offers some insight into Israeli perceptions of Arabs and of themselves. It is also an emotional account of Zionist interpretations regarding the creation of Israel and of the continued warfare with the surrounding Arab nations. Nowhere in the novel does Lev question the basic tenets of Zionism, nor does he recognize the national demands of the Palestinians.

The failure to come to grips with these issues has been a shortcoming of other Israeli accounts. More recently, *The Longest War: Israel in Lebanon*, an elegantly written personal memoir of the 1982 Israeli invasion of Lebanon by Jacobo Timerman, has been criticized by Palestinians and some Israelis for its unquestioning acceptance of the historic distortions and fallacies popularized by the Zionists.[9]

Timerman eulogizes the old-guard Labor Party leadership of Ben-Gurion, Meir, and Peres while asserting that the 1982 invasion of Lebanon was Israel's first aggressive war. Timerman is either unaware of or refuses to recognize the historical facts behind Israel's collusion with Britain and France that led to the 1956 tripartite (Israel, Great Britain and France) invasion of Egypt. He also reiterates the well-worn Israeli invectives against the Palestinians. As a popular writer who was persecuted and tortured for his opposition to the Argentine dictatorship, Timerman is in a unique position to recognize and empathize with the suffering of the Lebanese, but he fails to acknowledge a similar suffering among Palestinians. Because of his narrow historical view, Timerman, although sensitive to the horrors of the 1982 war, fails to deal with the depth of domestic Israeli opposition to the war or to the necessity for some sort of accommodation with the Palestinians. However, Timerman's moving descriptions of the appalling suffering generated by the 1982 war and his censure of the Begin government elicited criticism from conservative, pro-Begin forces. Thus in spite of their sensitivity to some of the contradictions

---

[9]Jacobo Timerman, *The Longest War, Israel in Lebanon*, New York: Alfred A. Knopf, 1982. See the reviews by Elia T. Zureik (a Palestinian) and Daniel J. Amit (an Israeli) in *Arab Studies Quarterly*, Spring, 1983.

within Israeli society, Lev and Timerman fail to come to grips with the Israeli determination to abrogate Palestinian national rights.

As with adventure novels, the Middle East has also been the setting for countless romantic or Gothic novels. The treatment of the Arab and/or Muslim world is identical in virtually all of them. The Arab world is an exotic, bizarre or mysterious backdrop. The Western, usually American, heroine is buffeted about in this sometimes beautiful but completely foreign world until she is invariably rescued by a charming, young and, generally, Western male. These novels have titles like *The House in the Kasbah*, *The Curse of the Kings* or *The Heart and the Scarab*. Their covers entice prospective readers, mostly Western women, with promises of an "Arabian Nights palace in Lebanon," "Mahmoud the handsome Egyptian professor," "a most exotic novel of romantic suspense."[10]

Novels of this genre generally do not present slanted political views—indeed, politics is entirely absent—nor do they usually contain overt racially biased stereotypes. However, at the very least, the theme of the Western man rescuing the innocent Western woman is highly ethnocentric and chauvinistic if not blatantly racist. For example, in *The House in the Kabash* the innocent American heroine, Paula, attempts to claim her inheritance of a vast Moroccan palace. In the process she is thwarted by complicated Moroccan law, surly servants and several young men including an Arab lawyer. Following a myriad of near disasters, Paula finds a cache of stocks and bonds hidden in the palace. She also discovers that the young man to whom she is most attracted is actually an Interpol agent who saves her from death at the hands of crooks who want the hidden bonds. The heroine in these novels may be adventurous and well-educated, but in times of crisis it is the charming male hero who saves her from the evils that befall

---

[10]Examples include: Maxine Reynolds, *The House in Kasbah*, New York: Beagle Books, 1972; Victoria Holt, *The Curse of the Kings*, Greenwich, Conn: Fawcett, 1973; Marguerite Kloepfer, *The Heart and the Scarab*, New York: Avon, 1981; Mary Stewart, *The Gabriel Hounds*, Greenwich, Conn: Fawcett, 1967.

her in the Arab world. In the best of these novels, such as *The Gabriel Hounds* by Mary Stewart, the descriptions of history and background have the ring of authenticity. *The Gabriel Hounds* is largely based on the life of Lady Hester Stanhope, and Stewart, known for her realistic recreations of locales, has clearly studied Lebanon, where the novel takes place, in some detail. In Stewart's novel an adventurous young Englishwoman visits her aunt in what is described as an "Arabian Nights palace in Lebanon." Once there she is terrorized and threatened with death. Ultimately her cousin, with whom she falls in love, is instrumental in rescuing her. With such emphasis on the mystery and strangeness of the locale, romantic novels contribute to the perpetuation of a distorted picture of the Middle East.

In another type of popular fiction, Western dependency on Arab petroleum is a major theme. Novels such as *On the Brink* and *The Crash of '79* revolve around international financial speculations and boycotts or price increases of Arab oil. In Paul Erdman's *The Crash of '79*, the Arabs use their natural resource to blackmail the West. The Israelis counter by dropping atomic bombs on Middle Eastern oil fields. After contaminating these fields, and in spite of the collapse of the world banking system, the Israelis emerge as the victors.

Erdman dismisses the Arabs as both "lazy ex-nomads" and crafty manipulators in matters of money.[11] In these examples Erdman has repeated the recurrent but illogical juxtaposition of laziness with crafty manipulation. On the one hand, sloth implies intellectual slackness; on the other hand, crafty manipulation implies energy and shrewdness. Because they are essentially emotional responses based on shallow or nonexistent knowledge, racial stereotypes often embody contradictory and false concepts. When stereotypes have been popularized over long periods of time, writers and others will sometimes use them without any thought as to their origin or impact. Contemporary novelists may use these

---

[11]Paul E. Erdman, *The Crash of '79*, New York: Pocket Books, 1976, p. 121, p. 55.

stereotypes, not out of political or ideological commitment, but simply because they are a convenient shortcut to characterization. However, the fact that novelists so casually resort to racist stereotypes indicates the pervasive nature of anti-Arab attitudes in Western society.

The action in *On the Brink* by Benjamin and Herbert Stein is built around the upheaval allegedly caused by increased petroleum prices, with concomitant spiraling inflation and depleted oil reserves. The Iranian and Arab members of OPEC are depicted as wily oil magnates who care nothing about the economic well-being of the world. Instead, they are interested in retribution for personal slights received in the West. The Saudi delegate, described as a "short, dark, clumsy, rich stranger,"[12] imagines how sweet the revenge will be.

In an unusual display of Muslim unity, the Iranians and Saudis propose an increase in petroleum prices. Excited by the proposal, the other OPEC members quickly express their support. The implication is that Muslim nations can only unify for actions that will harm Western interests. The chasm between the Muslim world and the West is subtly emphasized with the suggestion that had most of the OPEC delegates not been Muslim, prices would not have increased and "it would have been an occasion for breaking out champagne" (p. 22).

One exuberant OPEC delegate, who presumably represents Third World attitudes, asks, "Does this mean that the Zionist racist swine are going to be thrown into the sea?" (p. 22). The assumption of the novelists is that all Arab, Muslim and Third World leaders have racist attitudes toward Israel and that they are all equally hostile to the Western world. In *On the Brink* the petroleum-rich Arab and Muslim nations attempt to bring about the complete collapse of the Western world. The writers assume that the Western reader, steeped in preconceptions about the Arab world, will readily accept the idea that Muslim nations, united

---

[12]Benjamin Stein and Herbert Stein, *On the Brink*, New York: Ballantine Books, 1977, p. 24.

under the Prophet's banner, will eagerly wage full-scale economic war against their Western/Christian enemies.

Historically it was, of course, the predominantly Catholic nation of Venezuela that initiated the first round of OPEC price increases; however, historical errors and omissions are all too common in popular novels. Thus in *On the Brink* only the Ecuadoran delegate warns that price increases will cause an inflationary spiral that would result in global suicide. As he predicts, the prices in the United States and the rest of the world rise to such an extent that a simple taxi ride costs thousands of dollars. Not surprisingly, the average American vainly strives to maintain his standard of living. Meanwhile, all the available gold is being bought by an unnamed purchaser. In a nightmare scenario, extreme parties on the right grow in popularity. Violence breaks out in major cities and thousands are killed. The novel implies that the entire crisis is due to Arab/Muslim greed and desire for revenge. Finally, it is revealed that China has been the mysterious gold purchaser, but it will resell the gold in exchange for wheat from the United States. As the United States regains its economic ascendancy, the OPEC nations are forced to lower petroleum prices.

In a final scene the Ecuadoran OPEC delegate urges the Saudi Arabian representative never again to raise prices. However, the Saudi remains unconvinced and prefers to "keep an open mind" (p. 277). There is no such doubt for the reader. The conclusion is that the Arabs and Muslims were solely responsible for the disaster that was only averted by the fortuitous (and wildly improbable) assistance of the Chinese, who emerge as heroes. In the narrative, the Arabs not only bring the world to the brink of calamity, they fail to learn from the debacle. The Arabs emerge as the enemies who should never be trusted by the Western world. Indeed, the reader is left with the impression that the petroleum-rich Arab nations should be brought firmly under the control of the industrialized West. These fictionalized renditions severely distort the actual bilateral symbiotic or mutually dependent nature of the petroleum-exporting countries and the large multi-national companies. Nor do they take into account the massive recycling of so-called petrodollars into Western economies. Current estimates place Arab holdings in U.S. banks at $200 to $400 billion. As the events of the Iranian crisis so clearly indicated, these investments are vulnerable to U.S. controls, particularly the freezing of assets. In vivid contrast to fictional horror stories, the last decade has demonstrated the vulnerability of Arab oil economies. Finally, the failure of all the Arab oil exporters to use whatever economic power they had to alleviate the situation in Lebanon during the 1982 invasion amply demonstrated the limits of using economic leverage in lieu of political, diplomatic and military strategies.

The theme of the alleged religious fanaticism of petroleum-rich Muslims is also echoed in the novels *Jihad* and *The Clash of Hawks*. The title *Jihad* immediately foretells a story line involving a Muslim holy war against the West. Interestingly, *Jihad* is also the title of an espionage novel by Isser Harel. The cover of Geoffrey Clarkson's *Jihad* shows piles of money and a flag with a crescent and a scimitar, which are obviously meant to symbolize Islam. The novel is described as "Islam in a Holy War against the West: The Weapon—Our Money!"[13] In addition to its anti-Arab and Muslim theme, *Jihad* is blatantly racist in its treatment of Arabs and Iranians. Iranians are described as "loutish," the Arabs as "bloody," fanatical, looking all alike, greedy and lazy. Failing to distinguish between Arabs and Iranians is a common error in the West. Arabs are Semitic people speaking Arabic, while Iranians are Indo-Europeans who speak Farsi. Both are predominantly Muslim and share some cultural affinities, but remain distinct entities. There are also the usual contradictions found in such racial stereotypes. The Saudis are characterized as threatening world finance and as being "more used to herding goats and driving camels than to corporate finance" (p. 52).

In a complete misrepresentation of Arab culture, Clarkson cites the fairly commonplace event of men walking hand-in-hand as evidence of pervasive homosexuality. There is generally more

---

[13]Geoffrey Clarkson, *Jihad*, New York: Tom Doherty, distributed by Pinnacle, 1981. Clarkson may be a pseudonym, as the book is copyrighted by A.G. Yulin.

open physical contact among males in the Middle East than in Western societies. However, this is a cultural phenomenon and does not necessarily reflect sexual preference.

Islam is depicted as a dogmatic, hate-filled religion. One character in *Jihad* sees the Iranian revolution and Ayatollah Khomeini as typifying "the immemorial need of Allah for revenge" (p. 134). Repeating the theme, the British mystery writer Robert Charles mistakenly notes in *A Clash of Hawks* that the PLO and others have provoked fury and called for holy war. However, he also writes of "endless, merciless reprisal raids" led by Israel into southern Lebanon.[14] In *A Clash of Hawks* the Israelis eventually take over the Sinai with its newly discovered oil fields, but are prevented from detonating atomic bombs at the last moment by the dramatic intervention of the United States.

These novels are essentially predicated upon several crucial assumptions regarding the Middle East. First, the region is seen as an exotic backdrop for a wide variety of fiction. Arab and Iranian societies are distorted and maligned. Islam is not only consistently denigrated, but is also labeled as a violent, fanatical religion. Reflecting and reinforcing popular Western images regarding the conflict, the novelists do not refer to Israeli violence or extremism. Little mention is made of either actual or fictional Israeli raids or violence against the Palestinians and Arabs. Nor is the largely secular nature of the Palestinian liberation movement discussed. Indeed, the novels generally insinuate that Palestinian and Arab opposition to Israel is based upon narrow religious motivations.

In fact, Israel has launched numerous unwarranted attacks during its short history. For example, in 1953 the residents of Kafr Birim were forced to leave their homes, which were then completely destroyed; in 1954 the Christian cemetery in Haifa was desecrated; and in October 1956 the Israeli military massacred a number of villagers from Kafr Qasem as they returned home from the fields. These were not isolated incidents but formed part of a

---

[14]Robert Charles, *A Clash of Hawks*, New York: Pinnacle Books, 1975.

recurring pattern. However, because until 1982 such incidents were not publicized in the Western media, the public has remained largely unaware of Israeli-perpetrated violence. Consequently, Zionist interpretations of history are assumed to be valid and Israel is depicted as a positive, pro-Western ally. These assumptions, both in terms of a generally hostile portrayal of the Arabs and the Islamic world and a positive portrayal of Israel, are the basis for a huge number of espionage and mystery novels based on Middle Eastern themes.

VI. NOVELS: MYSTERY AND ESPIONAGE

An extraordinary number of novelists have utilized the dramatic possibilities posed by espionage activities in the Middle East. Authors of these "super thrillers," as they are often advertised, create myriad plot variations using Americans and Israelis as protagonists, and Arabs and Russians as villains. Since the Middle East conflict is international in scope, the authors can realistically spread the action of the plots over the entire globe. Using the Arab-Israeli conflict as a basis for story lines enables novelists to draw upon Western stereotypes about the Arab world, its society, people and geography. The prevalent view of the region is of an exotic, sexually charged atmosphere peopled with anti-Arab and anti-Islamic stereotypes which have evolved out of superficial, if not fallacious, information regarding both Arabs and Islam. Owing to their former imperial domination over most of the Middle East, the British and the French—in contrast to the average American— may generally possess a deeper historical knowledge of the region; however, by and large, European attitudes toward the area are much the same as American ones. Because the average Westerner already possesses this imaginary picture of the Middle East, fictionalized accounts dealing with the mystery and intrigue of the area are highly marketable.

Literally dozens of these spy and mystery novels are available wherever paperback books are sold. Many are jacketed in eye-catching covers which not infrequently depict stereotyped, evil-looking Arabs. The mass media have projected these images so often that the publishers do not have to add explanations. It is assumed that readers will realize that the villainous Arab is terrorizing innocent people.

In other novels, anti-Arab themes appear unexpectedly and completely unannounced. The cover jacket and plot summary of

The Vatican Target by Barry Schiff and Hal Fishman give no indication that the entire novel is replete with anti-Arab images. *Messages from Absalom* by Anne Armstrong Thompson revolves around the defection of a Soviet agent. In the last quarter of the novel, Arab terrorists, particularly one voluptuous female killer, suddenly appear. In *Lying There*, a Father Dowling mystery by Ralph McInerny, there are passing, almost gratuitous references to "terrorist fanatics," "some goddam Arab," and anti-Zionist radicals.[1] Often terrorists are portrayed in these novels as the "natural" product of Arab and Islamic culture. The anti-hero in *Kamal* is the terrorist son of a Palestinian refugee and a French woman. Similarly, in Ken Follett's *On Wings of Eagles* Iranians "appear as revolutionary dimwits, frantic tribesmen, crooks or disorganized bureaucrats."[2]

The plots in *Jihad* by Isser Harel and *Khamsin* by Menachem Portugali center around dramatic events in the Middle East. Portugali is, as mentioned in the preceding chapter, a pseudonym for two Israeli writers. *Khamsin* is set in Saudi Arabia; the villains are Russians and Arabs. Not surprisingly, these Israeli writers perpetuate the image of Israeli superiority partly by means of anti-Arab stereotypes. As former chief of Israel's secret service, Harel is particularly well-qualified to write an espionage novel. In brief, the plot in *Jihad* revolves around a Palestinian scheme to incite a full-scale Middle East war by bombing Mecca from an Israeli jet. The plan comes perilously close to succeeding, but is foiled because the hero has actually been an Israeli agent from the very beginning. Harel's characterizations are well-drawn, and he uses his knowledge of the Palestinian organizations to good effect. It is, however, unthinkable in this schema that the Palestinians should achieve any of their goals. In the end, all of the plotters are either dead or under Israeli detention. In the final analysis, the novel imparts the message that in spite of the alleged Arab willingness to perpetrate

---

[1] Ralph McInerny, *Lying There*, New York: Charter, 1979, pp. 11-12.

[2] Stephen Franklin book review, *Detroit Free Press*, October 5, 1983, of Ken Follett, *On Wings of Eagles*, New York: Morrow, 1983.

any barbarity, no matter how heinous, in order to gain their ends, the schemes will fail because Israel has superior military and intelligence forces. The right of Israel to use any means to achieve its goal and to destroy the PLO is also implicit within each of these story lines.

The specter of a nuclear conflagration touched off by a Middle East conflict has become another popular subject for writers of espionage novels. Potential nuclear disaster forms the focal point in *The Masada Plan, The Apocalypse Brigade, The Last of Days* and *The Fifth Horseman.* In *The Masada Plan* by Leonard Harris the Israeli secret services are the victors. The heroine, a worldly television newsperson, has been having a long-term affair with an urbane Israeli diplomat. Through a series of calculated leaks she discovers that the Israelis have atomic capabilities that they are willing to use. The title *The Masada Plan* suggests the Israeli determination to fight until death. In this instance, the Israelis seek to demonstrate to the world, particularly to the United States, their determination to survive even at the risk of nuclear holocaust. Because most of the plot's action takes place in the United States, the Middle East and the Arabs seem peripheral to the reactions of the West. In the conclusion of the novel there is some ambiguity as to whether the Israelis would actually have detonated their atomic bombs, which they had apparently planted in a number of major cities around the world.

The premise of the novel is that, although the use of nuclear bombs is undesirable, the development, possession and potential use of such weapons by Israel is understandable. The novel highlights the alleged willingness of Israelis to destroy themselves and others if the nation is threatened. The reader is left with the impression that the international community, particularly the United States, should not condemn Israel, but rather, understanding its unique history, single it out for favorable treatment.

Similarly, the intrigue behind the development of Israeli nuclear power is the theme of *Triple* by Ken Follett. Follett is an expert at creating fast-paced, tension-filled plots. *Triple* was an immediate number one best-seller. Although the publisher's note asserts that it is totally a work of fiction, *Triple* is actually a romanticized adventure that closely mirrors the Israeli uranium theft described in *Operation Uranium Ship*. The plot is predicated on the assumption that Arab nations, in this case Egypt, should never be permitted to develop nuclear capabilities. Conversely, it is assumed that it is permissible, perhaps even desirable, for Israel to be the only nuclear power in the region. The Egyptians, *fedayeen* terrorists (Palestinians are not mentioned by name) and the Soviet Union are the villains who are trying to obtain uranium for the development of a so-called "Arab bomb." Through a complex series of ruses culminating in the theft of the uranium, the Israeli secret service, Mossad, in cooperation with several sympathetic Europeans, foils the attempt and—almost incidentally—paves the way for the development of an Israeli nuclear bomb. Characters in the Harris and Follett novels do not question either Israel's moral right to develop a nuclear capability or its right to use nuclear weapons whenever or wherever it deems necessary.

The plot of Alfred Coppel's *The Apocalypse Brigade* centers on a complex interweaving of Arab radicals and fanatics, an Israeli decision to launch a "pre-emptive" attack, and an attempt by a conservative U.S. financier to force the development of synthetic fuels by spraying the Gulf oil fields with radioactive rain. Coppel's treatment of the Arabs and Muslims is entirely negative. When describing Arabs his favorite adjectives appear to be "swarthy" and "voluptuous."[3] Arab society is characterized as in the grip of terrorism, as living in "a self-induced trance of fantastic happenings and nonexistent successes" (p. 92), or as "having no culture meaningful to our time" (p. 271). In spite of his own use of sweeping, if not gross, generalizations, Coppel criticizes Arab society for its "typical Arab hyperbole" (p. 91). The narrative also constantly alludes to evil Palestinian leaders, the alleged prevalence of homosexuality in Arab society, and hordes of Arab or Muslim terrorists. From describing all Arabs as having the same physical

---

[3]Alfred Coppel, *The Apocalypse Brigade*, New York: Holt, Rinehart and Winston, 1981; Charter books, 1983, pp. 23, 27, 140.

characteristics to emphasizing the alleged weakness of the society, Coppel exhausts the entire grab bag of anti-Arab stereotypes and comes up with a totally negative interpretation. Individualized, sympathetic Arab characters do not exist in Coppel's schemata. Similarly, he demonstrates a marked ignorance regarding the richness and complexity of Arab and Islamic history. For example, by using carefully selected passages from the Quran, Coppel attempts to emphasize the alleged "innate" violence of Islam. Of course, similarly misleading conclusions could be reached from particular verses in most holy books. Nor is there any attempt to put these passages into their proper religious or historical contexts. When compared to other novels of the same genre in which anti-Arab stereotypes are common, *The Apocalypse Brigade* stands at the far end of the spectrum for its extreme and racially biased narrative.

Larry Collins and Dominique Lapierre, authors of four other best-selling novels, collaborated on *The Fifth Horseman*, a tale of Muammar Qaddafi's threat to start a nuclear war and Menachem Begin's steadfast refusal to yield to terrorist demands. *The Fifth Horseman* became an instant best-seller and was excerpted in *People* magazine. Avon purchased the paperback rights for $1.5 million and Paramount acquired the film rights.

Citing an anonymous State Department official, *People* touted the novel's plot as entirely plausible.[4] According to the article in *People* the Qaddafi character in *The Fifth Horseman* was based in part upon a CIA psychological profile which allegedly concluded that "the Libyan is not mentally unbalanced within the context of his own society."[5] Neither the CIA nor Collins and Lapierre note that for many Libyans Qaddafi is a genuinely charismatic leader. His determination to prevent Libya from being dominated by either the United States or the Soviet Union has won him support at home. In addition, he has directed a large portion of the nation's

---

[4]*People*, September 8, 1980. Larry Collins and Dominique Lapierre, *The Fifth Horseman*, New York: Simon and Schuster, 1980.
[5]*Ibid.*

petroleum revenues toward popular programs of domestic development, particularly in the fields of agriculture and education. For at least some in the Muslim world, Qaddafi's particular brand of Islamic fundamentalism and economic socialism presents an attractive example of a leadership that has continued to adhere to traditional Islamic social and religious values while simultaneously adopting many aspects of Western technology. Drawing on the CIA report, Collins notes that "for a Bedouin, peace may not be a desirable state." Clearly, the authors of popular novels are not the only ones to indulge in sweeping and distorted generalizations. The CIA report and *The Fifth Horseman* offer provocative examples of reality mirroring fiction and fiction simultaneously mirroring another fantasy.

Libya is not completely homogeneous in population; the Bedouin actually comprise an increasingly small portion of the society. More important, the Western concept of Bedouin society as being constantly at war has been largely refuted. For example, the anthropological studies in *The Desert and the Sown: Nomads in Wider Society* document the continued *interdependency* between Bedouin and agricultural societies.[6] Both have traditionally provided specific goods and services for one another. Conflict was not the norm and was generally caused by crisis (i.e., drought, disease) and the resulting scarcity of goods, or by one sector seeking to expand at the expense of the other. In addition, the conclusion drawn by the CIA and Collins and Lapierre appears to rest upon the highly questionable assumption that Bedouin society is somewhat more warlike and less peace-loving than any other society. In light of recent Western history this is, at best, a tenuous conclusion. If CIA reports, which are supposedly the product of long in-the-field research and expert opinion, contain such basic distortions and misleading conclusions, it is not suprising that the

---

[6]See Cynthia Nelson (ed.), *The Desert and the Sown: Nomads in the Wider Society*, Berkeley: Institute of International Studies, University of California, 1973.

United States has had some spectacular foreign policy failures in the Middle East.

Andrew Osmond's *Saladin!* provides a more objective picture of the conflicting forces and peoples in the Middle East. From Great Britain, Osmond uses first-hand experience in the Middle East to good effect. His protagonist, a former officer in the British Special Air Service, is engaged to lead "Saladin," the code name for a sabotage operation within Israel. The motivations of the characters in Osmond's novel, like those in Eric Ambler's *The Levanter*, are generally more complex than those of the two-dimensional figures in the previously cited novels. Both Osmond and Ambler have created characters who operate from a variety of incentives. Some Israelis work out of a commitment to and hope for peace; some murderous Arabs are bent only on revenge, but in Osmond's work in particular there are also thoughtful, highly educated Arabs who want to break the cycle of escalating violence. Initially Osmond's protagonist is the willing implementor of Saladin's daring scheme to blow up the newly constructed Israeli intelligence building (which has been ill-disguised as a post office). As the action progresses, the hero, who is caught by the Israelis, alters the plan so as to abort the original mission.

In the narrative Osmond focuses on a pair of killers, one Israeli and one Palestinian, and on a pair of essentially ethical individuals, again one Israeli and one Palestinian. The latter are caught in a web of events from which there is no escape. Rather like tragic figures, they are ultimately destroyed by their own better impulses. Osmond, whose hero returns to the bucolic English countryside, concludes that there is no possible resolution to the conflict. The narrative ends on a grim note:

> *No moderate Palestinian leader is in sight; Arafat's star is in the ascendant, Hussein's on the decline. Israel drives a hard bargain; the Arabs have the oil.*[7]

---

[7]Andrew Osmond, *Saladin!*, New York: Doubleday, 1976; Bantam, 1979, p. 346.

Osmond's hero judges that both sides are culpable and that the PLO, led by Yasser Arafat, is an entirely radical force. As Westerners, Osmond and the hero of *Saladin!* have the luxury of being able to stand apart from physical and emotional involvement in the conflict. The assumption is that the Western world is a superior one. From that position of superiority Osmond reasons that although both sides have rights and legitimate grievances, their stubbornness and tenacious determination to cling to the past have made a rational (one might even read *Western*) compromise impossible. Barring such a compromise, the conflict will drag on and more people on both sides will suffer and die. Osmond's protagonist, like most Westerners, returns to the safety of the Western landscape and dismisses the problem. In effect, the hero closes the narrative by saying "a plague on both your houses."

In striking contrast to the Osmond novel are the bulk of the espionage novels. *Phoenix*, *The Aleph Solution*, *Arafat is Next!* and *The Damascus Cover* are typical examples of the genre. The author of *Phoenix*, Amos Aricha, is assisted by Eli Landau, a prolific writer on Israeli subjects, who provides information on the Israeli government and secret services. In *Phoenix*, which enjoyed extensive sales and wide distribution throughout the United States, the plot revolves around the attempted assassination of Moshe Dayan. The Arabs are presented in a thoroughly unfavorable light, except for the Egyptians, who are described as not belonging to the Arab world. Ironically, prior to President Sadat's visit to Jerusalem in 1977, Egypt was depicted in popular writing as the cornerstone of that world.

All of the Arab characters in *Phoenix* are inept, venal and brutal. The assassin hired by the Libyans, who are portrayed as having limitless financial resources, is a Westerner of uncertain national origin. Although he aims to assassinate a ranking Israeli official, the assassin gradually comes to admire Jewish culture and Israeli professionalism. He also despises the Arabs for being bumbling, ineffectual amateurs. As a cool, calculating professional he cannot help admiring the technical skills and cultural richness of Israeli society.

In *The Aleph Solution*, by Sandor Frankel and Webster Mews, the brave and admirable Israeli commando foils a Palestinian attempt to take over the United Nations and hold the world hostage. Given the overwhelming support the cause of Palestinian self-determination enjoys in the United Nations, this scenario is highly improbable. Howard Kaplan in *The Damascus Cover* writes of brutal and inhumane Syrians. Like other novelists, Kaplan emphasizes the purported prevalence of homosexuality and eroticism in the Arab world. He denigrates Islam with caustic one-liners, as when he describes the call to prayer as a "banshee cry of the *muezzin*."[8] These clichés are reminiscent of the ethnic jokes some stand-up comics resort to for quick laughs and bear little or no relationship to reality.

The cover of *Arafat is Next!* features a caricature of Arafat in kaffiyah and dark sunglasses flanked by two robed Arabs carrying machine guns. Lionel Black, the author, is actually a pseudonym for an English biographer. Using skyjackings and the 1970 Jordanian civil war as a backdrop, he spins an action-packed plot based on the attempted assassination of Arafat by the friends of a British secret agent who has been accidentally killed by a Palestinian bomb. Although Palestinian attacks are roundly criticized, the activities of the Irgun in Palestine prior to 1948 are casually referred to as "the Irgun troubles."[9] Black fails to mention that these "troubles" included the bombing of the King David Hotel, assassinations (Lord Moyne, Count Bernadotte) and the massacre of women and children (Deir Yassin). As mentioned in Chapter IV, the Irgun and the Stern Gang operated from the basic assumption that violence would be necessary to secure the establishment of a Jewish state. Begin and Itzhak Shamir, his successor as prime minister, were both leaders in these terrorist organizations.

For Landau, Kaplan, Black and others, the Israelis are superior and there is little, if anything, to admire in Arab or Muslim civi-

---

[8]Howard Kaplan, *The Damascus Cover*, New York: Fawcett Crest Books, 1977, p. 7.

[9]Lionel Black, *Arafat is Next!*, New York: Stein and Day, 1975, p. 19.

lization. Israelis always triumph in these novels because they have moral right and Western civilization on their side.

In novels of espionage, as in the instant histories, Western intelligence services and governments generally cooperate with Israel. Even allegedly neutral characters, if they are portrayed in positive terms, assist Israel. In these novels, as in real life, Israeli intelligence services operate easily and independently within the United States. Indeed, the novelists clearly assume that domestic U.S. intelligence services have historically cooperated with Israeli intelligence agencies. Accepting the common Western stereotypes of the Arab world, the authors of these espionage thrillers assume that the readers will agree that any Israeli action, including terrorism and assassination, is acceptable in order to eradicate *Arab* terrorism. In real life, Palestinian leaders and some innocent bystanders have been victims of car and letter bombs and have been assassinated in Beirut and throughout Europe by Israeli agents.

With a few notable exceptions, the novels that present a more balanced or sympathetic image of the Arab world receive limited acclaim. Thomas Roberts' *The Heart of the Dog* is a rare fictionalized thriller that is sympathetic in its portrayal, not only of the Arab world, but of the issue of Palestinian self-determination. Roberts, a linguist with extensive experience in the Middle East, creates a Palestinian heroine who is described as a beautiful and caring human being. The Arab characters in *The Heart of the Dog* are a far cry from the usual two-dimensional stereotyped figures in most popular fiction. The hero, Deakon, a former CIA agent, is recruited as a decoy to discover why agents have been disappearing. Deakon journeys from North Africa to Beirut and through the refugee camps in Jordan. In the process he discovers that a Soviet tank with nuclear capabilities has been stolen by a small Palestinian liberation group. The Soviets, Israelis and others are all on the trail. As he maneuvers through a labyrinth of complications, Deakon establishes a warm friendship with a fiesty Arab from North Africa. He also consistently sees (as does the reader, through his eyes) the Palestinians in human, personalized terms. Deakon ultimately falls in love with Leila, a Palestinian woman who is not depicted as merely voluptuous, but as a complex, distinctive personality. Leila's mother had been killed in the Irgun massacre at Deir Yassin and she has joined the Palestinian liberation movement to achieve her national rights.

Throughout the novel, Roberts places the Palestinian cause within its correct historical context. His sophisticated use of Arabic reveals an expert knowledge not only of the language but of Arab culture in general. Roberts also correctly details the various splits within the PLO and its activities within Jordan prior to 1970. The narrative presents a sympathetic portrayal of the nature of the Palestinian struggle. In one particularly revealing passage, Deakon, having spent time with several Palestinian commandos, suddenly comprehends their motivations and goals:

> . . . This, I thought, was not a war I was going to. It was a revolution, and men went to die not as miserable herds of unwilling draftees who console each other with the age-old antics of army life, but as individuals whose decisions came from within. They were following through on their principles, and their attitudes were expectant resignation and mutual esteem.[10]

This is one of the few examples from contemporary novels in which the fictional account closely approximates the reality of the Palestinian struggle. As the Palestinian characters in the novel explain their dispersal from the land and describe the terrorist tactics of the Irgun, the historical tragedy, not just of the Israelis, but of the Palestinians as well, is revealed to the reader. Ultimately both Leila and Deakon's Arab friends are killed by the Israelis, who have been assisted by a leak at the CIA. As in *Saladin!*, the hero in *The Heart of the Dog* is a Westerner who becomes disillusioned. By the end of the novel, Deakon believes that a resolution to the Arab-Israeli conflict is unlikely; however, he ironically returns to Beirut to nurse his wounds and try to forget his failure at protecting those he loved.

---

[10]Thomas A. Roberts, *The Heart of the Dog*, New York: Random House,1982, p. 83.

In spite of its negative and essentially cynical conclusion, *The Heart of the Dog* renders a far more balanced account of the Arab world than most others of its genre. In addition, the novel gives the readers a rare glimpse into Palestinian and Arab lives. However, Roberts' novel appeared only in a hard-cover edition and enjoyed limited publicity and sales.

The Little Drummer Girl by John le Carré is a far more commercially successful espionage novel depicting the full scope of the tragedy surrounding the conflict between the Palestinians and the Israelis. Fans of le Carré will be delighted that he lives up to expectations in his first novel set in the Middle East. *The Little Drummer Girl* immediately rose to the top of the best-seller list. For many Westerners, particularly Americans, the novel will provide their first exposure in popular literature to the conflicting emotions and historical motivations of both Israelis and Palestinians.[11]

Israeli agents kidnap a fiesty English actress (Charlie), whom they persuade to help them infiltrate the PLO and capture the commander of a Palestinian terrorist network (Khalil). In order to get close to him, she is to impersonate the lover of his dead brother (Michel). Charlie falls in love with her tutor in undercover work (Gadi), Khalil's opposite number on the Israeli side, and with the image of Michel which Gadi creates to seduce her. Charlie is torn between the two sides in the conflict, and by the time she meets Khalil near the end of the novel we are prepared for him to be very much the same kind of man that Gadi is. They are brothers under the skin. The indoctrination Charlie has gone through prepares the reader for this turn, as Gadi has played the role of Khalil in order to make Charlie fall in love with Michel. On a deeper level Gadi and Khalil are alike or they would not be where they are. In the "theater of the real" where the actress is now perform-

---

[11] I am grateful to Michael Daher, a professor at Henry Ford Community College, for pointing this out in his unpublished review on *The Little Drummer Girl*, 1983. See also the review by John N. Gatch, Jr., *The Washington Report on Middle East Affairs*, Vol. 2, No. 1, April 18, 1983.

ing, different actors play opposite her, and her feelings become ambivalent. Like Charlie, the author also has ambivalent feelings about the Palestinians and the ongoing conflict between them and the Israelis.

Le Carré's mastery of espionage tactics is apparent in the intricately crafted plot and detailed descriptions of how Israeli agents infiltrate the PLO, forge passports and recruit personnel. However, as Charlie is sent to Beirut in order to penetrate Khalil's organization, she (and the reader) sees the poverty and suffering in the Palestinian refugee camps. She also comes face to face with committed Palestinians who are determined to gain restitution of their national rights.

Thus Charlie is torn between two masters. She is buffeted between guilt over the Holocaust, accompanied by a belief in Israel's unique history, and a growing sympathy for the dispossession and suffering of the Palestinians. While highlighting the Israeli struggle for security, le Carré also repeatedly notes the suffering of the Palestinians. The narrative emphasizes the disastrous human effects of the continued Israeli bombings of southern Lebanon. In a particularly prescient scene, le Carré vividly captures in words what actually occurred during the 1982 Israeli invasion of Lebanon.

> . . . And in the late spring at last . . . the long-awaited Israeli push into Lebanon occurred, ending that present phase of hostilities or, according to where you stood, heralding the next one. The refugee camps that had played host to Charlie were sanitised, which meant roughly that bulldozers were brought in to bury the bodies and complete what the tanks and artillery bombing raids had started; a pitiful trail of refugees set off northward, leaving their hundreds, then their thousands, of dead behind. Special groups eradicated the secret places in Beirut where Charlie had stayed; of the house in Sidon only the chickens and the tangerine orchard remained. The house was destroyed by a team of Sayaret, who also put an end to the two boys Kareem and Yasir. They came in at night, from the sea . . . and they used a special kind of American bullet, still on the secret list, that has only to touch the body to kill. Of all this—of the effective destruction of her brief love-affair with Palestine—Charlie was wisely spared all knowledge.[12]

---

[12]John le Carré, *The Little Drummer Girl*, New York: Alfred A. Knopf, 1983, p. 425.

As this passage indicates, for those intimately involved in the conflict—whether on the Israeli or Palestinian side—*The Little Drummer Girl* will probably be extraordinarily painful reading. The brutality and the deep commitment of both sides are clearly and realistically described. Israelis question their own motivations; Palestinians wonder about their leadership; and outsiders feel tormented by the validity of the conflicting national claims.

The Little Drummer Girl demonstrates that an extremely successful and dramatically exciting novel can also put the Israeli-Palestinian conflict in correct historical perspective. That the novel instantly became a best-seller was initially due to le Carré's well-deserved reputation as the contemporary master of the genre. However, the continued popularity of the book indicates that the public found its premise and presentation entertaining as well as believable. *The Little Drummer Girl* was subsequently made into a film starring Diane Keaton. Interestingly, the advertising campaign for the film made no mention of Israel or the Palestinians.

The well-publicized events of the 1982 war in Lebanon and the continued dispersal of the Palestinians served to reinforce the credibility of the novel. Le Carré, unlike so many other writers of commercially successful novels, does not resort to cheap innuendo or racial stereotypes. On the contrary, *The Little Drummer Girl* is all the more effective because of its three-dimensional characters. The Israelis and the Palestinians in the novel act out of rational, historically valid motivations. Neither side is denigrated or unrealistically glorified. It is a model of its genre that other writers would do well to emulate.

VII. CONCLUSION: INFLUENCES AND IMPACTS

The preceeding chapters demonstrate the pervasive negative character of the portrayal of Islam and Arabs throughout a wide variety of popular writing. These distorted images have been reiterated so frequently that they seem to reflect reality for many Westerners. The impact of these negative stereotypes has been particularly extensive because there are so few works in which the Arab world is depicted objectively, let alone favorably. Because there is almost no counterweight to this rendition of the Arab world and Islam, the average reader's perceptions of Arabs and Muslims are likely to be racially and religiously biased.

The relationship between reality and image has been explored by several well-known writers. Daniel J. Boorstin, a social historian, has noted that people in contemporary Western society may be in danger of confusing their illusions or images with reality. Technology—with its ability to publicize and reiterate images around the globe—has accelerated the process of creating and spreading illusions that assume the force of truth. Although referring to the creation of celebrities, Barbara Goldsmith, in an article in *The New York Times Magazine* entitled "The Meaning of Celebrity," has asserted that artificial images are often more vivid than real objects. As a result, according to Goldsmith,

> . . . *reality has become a pallid substitute for the image reality we fabricate for ourselves, which in turn intensifies our addiction to the artificial.*[1]

Indeed, these illusions are often so cleverly conceived that they are more easily accepted than reality.

---

[1] Barbara Goldsmith, "The Meaning of Celebrity," *The New York Times Magazine*, December 4, 1983, p. 76.

This ready acceptance of artificial images makes it possible for the media, including popular writing, to influence how individuals view specific ethnic groups. Historian Carlos E. Cortés has summarized the impact of the media on a culture's collective memory in the following terms:

> *The media have had a powerful influence on that memory, including how members of ethnic groups view their own past, how others view it, and how people view the significance of ethnic diversity in their nation's past, present and future.*[2]

That the public has little first-hand knowledge of the Middle East or its peoples, particularly Muslims and Arabs, has been well established. For most Americans, images and information about the Arabs or about people with Middle Eastern heritage have largely been gained from various electronic and print media. These images, as the case of popular writing clearly indicates, are often greatly distorted.

The portrayal of Arabs and Muslims in popular writing both influences and reflects their depiction in other media. Even a cursory glance at Western television, films, newspapers and magazines reveals an overwhelmingly hostile view of Arabs, uniformly described in subhuman terms rather than as individuals with both good and bad characteristics. Nor is Arab society and culture described in all its three-dimensional richness and complexity.

The creation of the "we-they" dichotomy is the foundation of what the columnist Richard Cohen has called "group-think." He points out that the separation of a particular ethnic, cultural, racial or religious group into a hostile, alien force is the "essence of prejudice."[3] Cohen has consistently warned against the tendency of mainstream American society to treat Blacks and Jews in this manner. Unfortunately, as has been demonstrated, numerous

---

[2]Carlos E. Cortés, "Historians and the Media: Revising the Societal Curriculum of Ethnicity." *Federation Reports* (Federation of Public Programs in the Humanities), Vol. IV, No. 1, January/February 1981, p. 9.

[3]Richard Cohen column, *Detroit Free Press*, February 27, 1984.

writers and journalists continue to engage in exactly this type of "group-think" against Arabs and Muslims.

The pervasive racist treatment of Arabs and Muslims in all forms of Western media augments its impact. This magnification of impact is referred to as *synergism*, a phenomenon in which the impact of the composite, and of each separate component, is greater than it would have been had they not interacted and reinforced one another. The stereotyping of Arabs in popular literature has an effect on that portion of the public that reads such material. The same treatment in textbooks, television, newspapers, magazines and films each has its own particular impact on the public; in addition, however, each medium enhances the effect of others. The constant repetition of these negative stereotypes of the Arabs and their culture reaches virtually every segment of the population. That almost every individual in Europe and North America has been exposed to these images has helped to create an underlying pre-disposition toward the adoption of specific political, economic, social and military policies toward the Middle East.

The unquestioning acceptance of these images has had a particularly important impact upon news coverage in the West. Many journalists, including John Cooley of ABC News, Georgie Anne Geyer, a syndicated columnist, and Trudy Rubin of *The Christian Science Monitor*, among others, have emphasized the problems of obtaining objective, balanced accounts of the Arab world. American journalists are often sent out to do "on the spot" stories and to become "instant" experts in times of crisis. Unlike many of their European counterparts who might cover the Middle East or another specific region for virtually all of their professional careers, U.S. journalists often do not have the time to become familiar with the languages, long histories and complex political nuances of a region. In such cases there is a danger that these reporters will fall back on the images that they have already assimilated. The ingrained attitudes—whether true or false—are then repeated without analysis or criticism.

This remains a problem even for European news specialists, who, because of the colonial history of the area, often have had longer, closer contacts with the Middle East. Peter Wilsher, foreign editor of the renowned London *Sunday Times* , has emphasized that the languages, religion, history, culture and political institutions of the Middle East are largely foreign to the West and that it has been difficult to find knowledgeable and non-partisan journalists to cover this crucial region. He points out that correspondents sent to the Middle East have to cope with ongoing danger,

> . . . *[seek] information, often from elusive, evasive, even aggressively antipathetic sources; write crisp, evocative prose on the basis of frequently imperfect data; and transmit it via some of the most ramshackle, unreliable communications equipment around.*[4]

In this regard, television news coverage has some particular problems. By the very nature of the medium, pictures are emphasized at the expense of analysis. Consequently, television news coverage, particularly in the United States, tends to be crisis-oriented. As the impact of television news has expanded, the nature of that news and its presentation have become highly controversial issues. It is generally estimated that over sixty percent of the American public use television as their major source of news. (Newspapers have simultaneously enjoyed an upswing in popularity.[5]) In the keen competition for higher ratings, news programming has become increasingly important; however, the tendency toward more subjective coverage and the emphasis on news personalities over objective journalism have been roundly criticized. Then, too, broadcasters, like print journalists, have noted that they are constantly pressured by a wide variety of interest groups and politicians who try to influence news coverage.

Certainly, coverage of Middle East issues is a major focal point for both subjectivity and outside pressures. Because of its vital strategic location and petroleum resources, the region is of pri-

---

[4]Peter Wilsher, "Getting to the heart of Arabia," *The Sunday Times*, August 15, 1982.

[5]"TV News Gets Bigger, But Is It Better?" *U.S. News and World Report*, February 21, 1983.

mary interest to the Western- and Eastern-bloc nations. In addition, the existence and continuation of an independent Israel has been a major U.S. policy concern. As the examples from popular books have indicated, Arab opposition—in particular, Palestinian Arab opposition—to Israel has been widely misunderstood and misrepresented in Western media. News coverage of the issue has been no exception to this trend.

Recently, media analysts and experts have themselves begun to grapple with this issue. "Blind Spot in the Middle East" by John Weisman deals directly with the problem of balance in news coverage of the Arab-Israeli conflict. This *TV Guide* feature stresses that U.S. networks have been more likely to present Israeli interpretations than Palestinian viewpoints. Editorial choices regarding Israel and the Arab world have been dubbed "the Great Touchy Issue"[6] that continues to influence television news. The coverage of the 1982 Israeli invasion of Lebanon and the subsequent debate surrounding it have placed this issue in even clearer perspective. Because of their bias toward Israel, many in the Western media initially accepted at face value the Israeli demands for a "25-mile buffer zone." During the same period, former secretary of state Alexander Haig used the collective "we" when referring to Israeli military successes.

An extensive review of news coverage during this critical time was published in the noted *Columbia Journalism Review*. In this article, Roger Morris emphasized that, initially, television news tended to echo Israeli calls to "clear-out," or "eliminate" the PLO from southern Lebanon; however, as the battles dragged on and Beirut was besieged, correspondents began to reassess their initial viewpoints. For many, this reassessment of Israeli actions was clearly a painful process. As Morris has so perceptively expressed it:

> . . . *There was also evident trauma for American reporters, many of whom seemed, for the first time, to be seeing the Palestinians in human terms. . . . As "the other side" took on human reality, reporters*

---

[6]John Weisman, "Blind Spot in the Middle East, *TV Guide*, October 24-30, 1981.

inevitably became sympathetic to the plight of the civilians. Added
to that was the shock of journalists like Chancellor and Farrell,
made evident by their allusions to Beirut in terms of Manhattan.[7]

"Human terms" and "the other side" are the operative expressions here. Just as writers of popular literature have dehumanized Arabs, so too have the rest of the Western media generally portrayed the Arabs as "the other side."

The news coverage of the siege of Beirut and the subsequent massacres at the Palestinian refugee camps of Sabra and Shatila raised a storm of protest from pro-Israeli and other groups within the United States. The war in Lebanon and its devastating impact on the Lebanese and Palestinian civilians heightened the awareness of many Westerners as to the human costs of Israeli actions. It also marked the first time that Israel had been covered in negative terms by the Western news media.

Until 1982 Israel had consistently put itself forward as morally superior to the surrounding Arab nations. The Western media had generally accepted this line without question. After the 1982 war, and particularly following the Sabra and Shatila massacres, Israelis were dismayed by the criticism and reassessment in much of the Western press, as it ran counter to the treatment they had become accustomed to receiving. Israel and its supporters immediately countered that the nation was being victimized by a double standard. They argued that Israel's actions were no worse than those of many other nations and that the media were exaggerating the negative consequences of the war.

Some of the dismay appeared to stem from the fact that the invasion and particularly the human costs of the war had been covered so extensively. In fact, the real problem resided in the historical representation of the Arab-Israeli conflict in the Western media. Prior to 1982, with very few exceptions, Israel had been

---

[7]Roger Morris, "Beirut—and the Press—under Siege," *Columbia Journalism Review*, November/December 1982, p. 33. A further discussion of specific news coverage of the 1982 war is found in "Israel's War on Lebanon in the Press," American-Arab Anti-Discrimination Committee, July 1982.

depicted in highly idealized terms, while in contrast, the Arabs had been viewed either as the faceless enemy or in negative stereotypes. Both representations had been greatly exaggerated. The idealized image of Israel was maintained for so many decades in part because of the overwhelmingly anti-Arab bias in the West.

That the events of 1982 contradicted both of these preconceived images proved to be difficult for many, particularly those in the media, to accept. Two columns in *The Washington Post* soon after the massacres epitomize the contradictory responses caused by changing perceptions of Israel and the larger conflict. George F. Will, who is well-known for his pro-Israeli stance, attempts to come to grips with the moral dilemma posed by the invasion of Lebanon and the massacres in the camps. Will repeatedly minimizes or even tries to deny Israel's role in the massacres. He goes on to characterize Israel as incarnating "the response . . . of intelligence to animalism."[8] Will appears to be primarily interested in relieving Israel of further criticism but not in investigating the motivations or root causes of Israeli actions.

In the same issue of the *Post*, but contrasting sharply with the Will analysis, Mary McGrory explores the responses to the events in Beirut. Entitled "After the Massacre, the See-No-Evil, Hear-No-Evil Excuses," the article pinpoints the dilemma posed by Israeli actions and denials. McGrory notes that Israel had historically put itself forward as a model, "a light among nations."[9] However, the 1982 war in Lebanon had brought the true proportions of the conflict and the suffering of both Israelis and Palestinians into sharper focus. In short, the 1982 invasion called into question the idealized image of Israel. McGrory's discussion is more incisive than that of Will, who attempts to maintain the distorted image of Israel while paying lip service to the suffering of the Arabs. The 1982 war may have marked a watershed year for a shift in attitudes regarding the Arab-Israeli conflict.

---

[8]George F. Will "Israel Should Show, 'A Decent Respect'," *The Washington Post*, September 23, 1982.
[9]Mary McGrory, "After the Massacre, the See-No-Evil, Hear-No-Evil Excuses," *The Washington Post*, September 23, 1982.

Certainly John le Carré's *The Little Drummer Girl*, which was published in 1983, contained a far more enlightened rendition of the Arab world than had heretofore been seen in popular fiction. That the novel remained on the best-seller list for many weeks was a tribute not only to le Carré's enormous talent, but also to the general public's receptivity to a more penetrating and three-dimensional presentation of both the Palestinians and the Israelis.

On the other hand, the 1984 publication of *The Haj* by Leon Uris clearly demonstrates the continued pervasiveness of anti-Arab stereotypes. If the novel had been directed against any other ethnic group it is doubtful that it would have been considered for publication. The media continue to use racist, anti-Arab images with impunity largely because until very recently there were no organized movements or groups that objected to the biased treatment of Arabs or Muslims. Indeed, Arabs remain the only major ethnic group which is still consistently defamed in the Western media. Doubleday, a publishing giant, launched *The Haj* with great fanfare and it was immediately chosen as both a Book-of-the-Month Club and Literary Guild selection. In this regard it is important to recall that Doubleday owns the Book-of-the-Month Club. However, the instant recognition of Leon Uris' name practically guaranteed that the novel would soar to at least number three on the best-seller list.

In spite of the commercial success of *The Haj*, reviewers almost unanimously condemned the novel. The critical disapproval of *The Haj* contrasted markedly to the acclaim accorded *Exodus*, which was also highly biased. There are several instructive reasons for the radically different critical receptions the two novels received.

In *Exodus*, the major characters, all Israelis or Western sympathizers, are portrayed in positive terms. Palestinians, referred to only as Arabs, are depicted in uniformly negative terms, but the focus of the novel remains on the Israelis. The Jewish Israeli characters in *Exodus* became the new—albeit positive—stereotypes. In contrast, the focus in *The Haj* is on the Arab characters. The Israelis are still depicted as entirely good, but they are peripheral to the action of the plot. The incessantly vituperative condemnation of the Arab world in *The Haj* strains the credulity of even the most gullible reader. In short, Uris has created such a totally intolerant and overtly hostile picture of the Arab world, that the novel fails to be believable.

Importantly, the critical reviews of *The Haj* also indicate a growing awareness that such biased and racist treatments of Arabs and Muslims are unacceptable. The widespread criticism of *The Haj* emphasizes that the Western public is beginning to recognize that much media coverage, including that in novels, has presented distorted and extremely misleading images of the Arab world. Ever-increasing segments of the public will no longer accept or agree with the biased, distorted versions of the Arab world that have been popularized by Uris and other novelists. Although the public has become more sensitive to the negative stereotyping of Arabs and Muslims, the publication and massive sales of *The Haj* demonstrate that the process of presenting factual, objective images of the Arab world is just beginning to make an impact. In this regard, it is instructive to glance, at least briefly, at the depictions of the Middle East in other media forms and how they mirror those in both the news and popular writing.

Because novels or themes based on story lines from popular writing are often made into films or television productions, there is a direct correlation of how the Middle East is portrayed in all three mediums. As previously noted, the film "Exodus," based on the novel of the same name, was an enormous box-office success. Paramount Pictures is reputedly going to produce *The Fifth Horseman*, about Libyans and Palestinians planting a nuclear bomb in New York City. The projected film, based on the Collins and Lapierre novel, is reminiscent of several other novels with similar plot lines. Popular television situation comedies and dramas frequently use stereotypical anti-Arab characters and plots.[10]

---

[10]For a more extensive discussion of the treatment of Arabs in films see: Laurence Michalak, "Cruel and Unusual: Negative Images of Arabs in Popular American Culture," *ADC Issues*, no. 19, January 1984; Jack G. Shaheen explores the portrayal of Arabs on television in; "The Arab Stereotype on Television," *The*

Television producers have also found docu-dramas based on the lives of certain political leaders from the Middle East to be popular with the American public. The four-hour docu-drama of Golda Meir's life, which closely paralleled her own autobiography, was a critical success. "Sadat," starring the Oscar-winning Louis Gossett Jr., was highly laudatory of the former Egyptian president; in contrast, the treatment of Gamal Abdul Nasser was almost a caricature in its two-dimensional, biased presentation. The depiction of Sadat after the Camp David accords as a good leader follows the pattern of popular writing during that time.

Generally speaking, after the Egyptian-Israeli peace treaty, Sadat and Egypt were both treated favorably by all Western media. Indeed, Egypt was increasingly viewed as unique and separate from the Arab world. Under Nasser's regime (1952-70) Egypt had been depicted as the cornerstone of Arab politics, playing a vital role in directing Arab society, culture and politics. However, following Sadat's peace initiatives, popular writers—reflecting Western politics and opinion—stopped depicting Egypt and Egyptians as part of the Arab mainstream. Egyptians were no longer continually described as swarthy, evil, or violent. In short, once Egypt recognized Israel and moved within the Western geo-political orbit, it became a "good guy," no longer subject to the opprobrium reserved for the Arab "bad guys." Sadat, with his close relations to the Western media, encouraged this stance.

Such protection of friendly individuals or sub-groups from the stereotyped treatment accorded to the larger out-group is fairly common. Just as individuals have been known to remark that a particular Black, Jew, Italian, Catholic, etc., is different from the rest of their ethnic, racial or religious group ("Some of my best friends are _____"), so too, did the Western media separate Egypt from the rest of the Arab world. Western society was, in fact, saying that since the Egyptians had become friends with

Link, Vol. 13, No. 2, April/May 1980 and *The TV Arab*, Bowling Green, OH: Bowling Green State University Popular Press, 1985.

Israel they could not be like the rest of the Arabs, who were still perceived in almost totally negative terms.

The removal of Egypt from the rest of the Arab world, by both the media and popular opinion in the West, contradicted historical and geo-political realities. In addition, such a separation implied that not only was the West no longer to view Egypt as part of the Arab world, but that Egyptians were no longer to consider themselves to be Arabs. In other words, the Egyptians were to deny their own identity and adopt one largely formulated and popularized by the West. Finally, treating Egypt as separate from the Arab world failed to confront the far larger and more crucial issue of the continued antagonism between the Western and Arab worlds. The approach implied that accommodation and understanding could only be attained if the Arabs repudiated their own identities. In part, opposition to Sadat originated in the Egyptian awareness that he had encouraged the West, particularly the media, to separate the nation from its Arab foundation.

The alarming tendency to recreate the Middle East in Western terms has also pervaded more serious academic works and textbooks. Scholars such as Michael Suleiman and Iyad al-Qazzaz and organizations such as the Middle East Studies Association have all investigated the bias against the Arabs and Islam contained in many American textbooks. Often these distortions have been based more upon preconceived ideas than upon scholarly research. Recently, academics have also begun to investigate such distortions in older studies. For example, *Through Foreign Eyes: Western Attitudes Toward North Africa* is a scholarly collection that examines the double standard that many Western academics have applied in research on North Africa.[11] This provocative work focuses on the imperial criteria that scholars traditionally have used when describing the cultures of North Africa; in addition, it is revealed that in the past writers have tended to emphasize the

---

[11]*Through Foreign Eyes: Western Attitudes Toward North Africa*, ed. by Alf Andrew Heggoy, Aurie H. Miller, James J. Cooke and Paul J. Zing, Washington, D.C., University Press of America, 1982.

superstitions and alleged cruelty of the region while failing to note similar phenomena in the Western world.

Even in academic works, the Arab and Islamic worlds are frequently portrayed in stereotyped and, therefore, fallacious terms. Peter A. Iseman highlighted the deleterious effects of these distortions in his short article, "The Middle East as a Desert and Mohammad as a Madman," in the *Saturday Review*. The title itself indicates Iseman's recognition of the prevalence of popular stereotypes about Muhammad and the Middle East. After assessing the historical development of these distorted images, Iseman points to the dangers posed by their perpetuation. In Iseman's words:

> . . . *For better or for worse, the geopolitical realities have changed, but the awareness that precedes understanding has yet to follow. The Moslem world is going to be on the front page and the editorial page for a long time to come. And as the American stake in the region increases, we can less and less afford "intelligence failures" that simply mirror a tradition of ignorance and misperception.*[12]

This failure of intelligence, which popular writing has in part created and helped to perpetuate, has had a number of specific effects in the domestic and international policies of the United States. Domestically, it has helped to foster a form of institutionalized racism toward Arab-American citizens and Arabs in general. This racism has taken the form of discrimination against individuals as well as more formal governmental policies. Publications and statements by organizations such as the Association of Arab-American University Graduates (AAUG), the American-Arab Anti-Discrimination Committee (ADC), and the American-Arab Affairs Council attest to the all-too-common discrimination against Arabs within American society. "Operation Boulder" during the Nixon Administration and "Abscam" during the Carter Administration are two relatively recent examples of governmental policies that were based upon anti-Arab prejudice.

---

[12]Peter A. Iseman, "The Middle East as a Desert and Mohammad as a Madman," *Eastern Review*, August 1976; reprinted from *Saturday Review*, May 29, 1976.

Likewise, U.S. politicians have frequently evinced anti-Arab biases based not so much upon political issues as upon hostility born of prejudice. Part of this is undoubtedly owing to the politicization of the Arab-Israeli conflict; however, on not infrequent occasions, U.S. politicians have far exceeded mere support for the Israeli side and opposition to the Arabs—hence former New York Mayor Wagner's refusal to greet a King of Saudi Arabia or the characterization of the PLO as "an international Ku Klux Klan" by another leading political figure. Particularly in presidential election years, the rhetoric, both in praise of Israel and excoriation of Arab nations, becomes extreme. The debate that surrounded the sale of AWACs to Saudi Arabia is another instructive example of the expression of anti-Arab sentiments. Political action committees (PACs) use direct pressure and influence, but rely upon a certain climate of opinion to create an atmosphere of support for their causes. This is nowhere more valid than regarding the PACs that favor increased U.S. support for Israel.

Politicians, lobbyists, PACs and others seeking to influence political policies employ many of the same misrepresentations that the writers of popular literature use to depict the Arabs and Islam. The use of such distortions is a regular feature of U.S. political life. That the society at large holds these stereotypes to be true considerably eases the task of those seeking to secure policies favorable to Israel. Conversely, it exacerbates the difficulties of those seeking to gain support for Arab nations or groups.

Arabs, even Arab Americans, remain largely outside U.S. political power circles. They are still largely viewed as "foreign"— different religiously, ethnically and culturally. In contrast, Israel is generally perceived, and depicted in popular culture, as part of the Western world. Not surprisingly, the ubiquitous anti-Arab stereotypes create an atmosphere that is highly favorable to pro-Israeli viewpoints.[13]

---

[13]A procovative analysis of the interrelationship of the anti-Arab and pro-Israeli attitudes within the United States from the European perspective is found in Thomas Ross, "Israel, Jews, and the Arabs," *World Press Review*, March 1984, p. 46; excerpted from *Frankfurter Allgemeine*.

Anti-Arab stereotypes and misrepresentations about the Arab and Muslim worlds have also affected various other U.S. governmental institutions. For example, several years ago a secret U.S. intelligence report leaked by Jack Anderson contained analyses of Yasir Arafat that were startlingly similar to descriptions in Kiernan's biography and other caricatures in popular fiction. The report allegedly stressed Arafat's appearance, including a discussion of his beard, dark glasses and uniforms, and his so-called insecure personality.[14] Such distorted, if not completely misleading, assessments were apparently similar to those intelligence reports on Qaddafi that were used as a basis for *The Fifth Horseman* by Collins and Lapierre.

As previously noted, a number of former agents, both from the United States and Israel, have subsequently turned their talents to writing fictional accounts of espionage exploits. According to Peter Maas, who is currently writing a "true-to-life thriller" on the underground activities of the noted agent Edwin P. Wilson, agents are also aficionados of espionage novels. Wilson has been convicted of a number of crimes involving illegal international activities. In his somewhat tongue-in-cheek article in *The New York Times Book Review* section, Maas delightedly points out that agents have been known to enjoy best-sellers such as Robert Ludlum's *The Parsifal Mosaic* and Ken Follett's *Triple*.[15] That the latter revolves around a plot to provide a nuclear bomb for Libya is particularly ironic in light of the fact that a number of Wilson's crimes involved activities in that country. However, Maas points out that John le Carré is conspicuously absent from the list of favorite authors. He wonders rhetorically whether perhaps le Carré's unglamorous, nondescript agents and morally ambiguous situations are too close to reality to provide amusement to real spies. Le Carré equal treatment of all secret services may also offend those who prefer to regard espionage wars simply as struggles of

---

[14]Jack Anderson column, *Detroit Free Press*, May 25, 1982.
[15]Peter Maas, "Guess Who Reads Spy Novels," *New York Times Book Review,* February 19, 1984.

"good guys" versus "bad guys." Perhaps it should not be surprising that intelligence agents rely on the same caricatures and stereotypes of the Arab and Islamic worlds in their work that writers use in their novels. This vicious circle of art imitating life imitating art has perpetuated negative stereotypes of Arabs.

Thus the highly favorable portrayal of Israel and the negative depictions of Arabs throughout all forms of Western media have contributed to the consistently pro-Israeli policies of the U.S. government. This is *not* to imply that these pro-Israeli and anti-Arab stereotypes have been the sole or even the most important influences on the formulation of U.S. policies. National self-interest, in the form of strategic, military, financial and international political considerations, forms the basis of U.S. foreign policy. So long as support for Israel appears to strengthen U.S. interests in the Middle East and elsewhere it will likely continue.

Clearly, it is outside the scope of this study to explore the nature, causes or results of U.S. foreign policy in the Middle East. However, it is pertinent to note that the favorable climate of public opinion toward Israel has facilitated and encouraged a consistently favorable U.S. foreign policy toward that nation. Conversely, the largely anti-Arab and anti-Islamic climate of opinion has encouraged and applauded anti-Arab stances by the U.S. government. It has also made cordial relations with Islamic nations such as Turkey, Pakistan and Iran more difficult. In addition, these negative attitudes have considerably complicated and even thwarted any pro-Arab U.S. policies. The anti-Arab, anti-Muslim stereotyping permeating Western media and culture has demonstrably contributed to costly errors of judgment in policies toward the Middle East.

As noted, the 1982 war in Lebanon seemed momentarily to alter popular perceptions regarding this crucial area. Increased political and social activity by Arab Americans and those interested in the Arab and Islamic cultures have also raised public awareness of the problem. However, because of the sheer pervasiveness of the negative stereotypes, and an equal or even greater number of glorified accounts of Israel, Western prejudices and misconceptions about Arabs, Muslims and the Middle East remain intact. Such deep-seated images can only be dispelled after protracted efforts to identify and then to eradicate the distortions and finally to replace them with more balanced, factual images. This book has been one such effort.

VIII. SUGGESTED SOURCES

The following is a brief bibliographic discussion of selected key sources which provide insights and basic information on various aspects of the Middle East and U.S.-Arab relations. The discussion is divided under major topical headings.

HISTORY

For a good general history of the region see Sidney Nettleton Fisher, *The Middle East*, third edition (New York: Alfred A. Knopf, 1979). See also Joseph J. Malone *The Arab Lands of Western Asia* (Englewood Cliffs, N.J., Prentice Hall, 1973). Godfrey Jansen in *Militant Islam* (New York: Harper and Row, 1979) presents a provocative discussion of contemporary Islam.

Two excellent studies that refute many of the fallacies regarding Arab women and Islam are: *Middle Eastern Muslim Women Speak*, edited by Elizabeth Warnack Fernea and Basima Qattan Bezirgan (Austin: University of Texas Press, 1977), and Nadia Haggag Youssef, *Women and Work in Developing Societies* (Berkeley: Institute of International Studies, University of California, 1974). George Antonius in *The Arab Awakening* (London: 1948, reprint Beirut: Khayats, n.d.) provides a straightforward description of the growth of Arab nationalism. Malcom Kerr's *The Arab Cold War, 1958-1964: A Study of Ideology in Politics* (New York: Oxford University Press, 1965) is a short but sophisticated analysis of inter-Arab politics. Kennett Love in *Suez: Twice Fought War* (New York: McGraw-Hill, 1969) and Donald Neff, *Warriors at Suez* (New York: The Linden Press, Simon and Schuster, 1981) are two of the best works on international intrigue and the 1956 Arab-Israeli war. Peter Mansfield in *Nasser's Egypt* (London: Penguin, 1965) presents a balanced account of Nasser and his revolutionary leadership of Egypt and the Arab world.

J.C. Hurewitz, *The Struggle for Palestine* (New York: Norton, 1950) and Harry Sacher, *Israel and the Establishment of the State* (London: G. Weidenfield and N. Colson, 1952) are both scholarly accounts of the establishment of Israel. Fred Khouri in *The Arab-Israeli Dilemma*, second edition (New York: Syracuse University Press, 1976) gives a complete and objective history of the conflict. *The Transformation of Palestine* edited by Ibrahim Abu-Lughod (Evanston: Northwestern University Press, 1971) contains several excellent studies on Palestine during the British mandate and on Palestinian demography and society. Edward H. Buerig in *The United Nations and the Palestinian Refugees* (Bloomington: Indiana University Press, 1971) examines the issue of the Palestinian refugees and the work of the United Nations.

On the formation and development of the Palestinian national movement both John K. Cooley in *Green March, Black September: The Story of the Palestinian Arabs* (London: Frank Cass, 1973) and William B. Quandt in *Palestinian Nationalism: Its Political and Military Dimensions* (California: The Rand Corporation, 1971) provide concise yet readable accounts. Both the *Journal of Palestine Studies* and *Arab Studies Quarterly* contain more detailed scholarly studies on specific historical and political Middle East topics.

STEREOTYPES: PREJUDICE AND RACISM

There is a large body of information on stereotypes, prejudice and racism; however, Gordon Allport's *On the Nature of Prejudice* (Cambridge, Mass: Addison-Wesly, 1954) remains one of the best. Kenneth E. Boulding's *The Image* (Ann Arbor: University of Michigan, 1956) is a pioneering work on the topic. Ole R. Holsti has written numerous quantitative studies on language and images. For example see his "The Belief System and National Images: A Case Study," *The Journal of Conflict Resolution*, no. 6 (1982). See Bruno Bettelheim and Morris Janowitz in *Dynamics of Prejudice* (New York: Harper and Row, 1950) for a discussion of racism, prejudice and stereotypes. See also G. Selznick and S. Steinberg, *The Tenacity of Prejudice* (New York: Harper and Row, 1969), for a well-reasoned analysis of the perpetuation of prejudicial attitudes.

Ralph Ellison in *Invisible Man* (New York: Random House, 1947; Vintage, 1972) deals with the issue of stereotypes and racism as it pertains to American society. Eric Sellin in "Alienation and Intellectual Invisibility of Algerian Nationals: The Writer's Vision," *Settler Regimes in Africa and the Arab World: The Illusion of Endurance*, edited by Ibrahim Abu-Lughod (Wilmette Illinois: Medina University Press International, 1974) deals with a parallel phenomenon in colonial Algeria.

Willard G. Oxtoby has explored the impact of language with particular reference to the Middle East in "The War of Words: a Look at the Literature," *America and the Middle East* (New Haven: Committee on the Middle East Crisis, March 1968). Edward Said's, *Orientalism* (New York: Pantheon, 1978) is a seminal and controversial discussion of the larger issue of Western perceptions of the Middle East over the last several hundred years. For a scholarly study of the specific impact of negative stereotypes of the Middle East in the United States, see Michael W. Suleiman, "National Stereotypes as Weapons in the Arab-Israeli Conflict," *Journal of Palestine Studies*, Vol. III, No. 3, Spring 1974.

MEDIA

Split Vision: The Portrayal of Arabs in the American Media, edited by Edmund Ghareeb (Washington: The American-Arab Affairs Council, 1983) is a complete exposition of western media treatment of the Arab world. The book includes first-hand interviews with media professionals and essays by scholars in the field.

The American Media and the Arabs, edited by Michael C. Hudson and Ronald A. Wolfe (Washington: Center for Contemporary Arab Studies, Georgetown University, 1980) and *The Arab Image in the Western Media*, 1979 International Press Seminar, (London: Outline Books, 1980) both provide insight into the problem of objective, knowledgeable news coverage of the region. Michael W. Suleiman in "An Evaluation of Middle East News Coverage in Seven American Newsmagazines July-December 1956," *Middle East Forum*, XLI (Autumn 1965) and Janice J. Terry in "The Western Press and the October War: A Content

Analysis," *Middle East Crucible*, edited by N.H. Aruri (Wilmette Illinois: Medina University Press International, 1975) provide quantitative analyses of coverage of specific conflicts. "Beirut— and the Press—under Siege," *Columbia Journalism Review*, November/December 1982 by Roger Morris is a timely investigation of the ongoing problems of providing objective news coverage.

For information regarding materials on the Middle East in U.S. high schools see: William J. Griswold, *The Image of the Middle East in Secondary School Textbooks* (New York: Middle East Studies Association, 1975), Michael W. Suleiman, *American Images of Middle East Peoples: Impact on the High School* (New York: Middle East Studies Association, 1977).

Jack Shaheen has written numerous articles on the stereotyping of the Arab world on television. These articles include "American Television: Arabs in Dehumanizing Roles," in the aforementioned *The American Media and the Arabs* and *The TV Arab* (Bowling Green, OH: Bowling Green State University Popular Press, 1985). William C. Adams deals with television coverage in *Television Coverage of the Middle East* (Norwood, NJ: ABLEX publishing, 1981). John Weisman described the problems of objectivity in "TV's Blind Spot in the Middle East: Why You Don't See More Palestinians on TV," *TV Guide*, October 24-30, 1981.

THE UNITED STATES AND THE MIDDLE EAST

William Quandt in *United States Policy in the Middle East: Constraints and Choices* (Santa Monica, California: Rand Corporation, 1970) traces U.S. policy from 1946 to 1969 and offers some suggestions for the future. *The Middle East: Quest for an American Policy*, edited by W.A. Beling (New York: Albany State University, 1973) explores the various options available to U.S. policy makers. Richard H. Curtiss in *A Changing Image: American Perceptions of the Arab-Israeli Dispute* (Washington: American Educational Trust, 1982) focuses on public attitudes and government policy. More specific studies of U.S. policy are found in John Snetsinger, *Truman, The Jewish Vote and the Creation of*

Israel (Stanford, California: Hoover Institution Press, 1974) and Robert W. Stookey, *America and the Arab States: An Uneasy Encounter* (New York: John Wiley and Sons, 1975).

IX. CITED MATERIALS: INCLUDING BIOGRAPHIES, "INSTANT HISTORIES" AND NOVELS

Agee, Philip, *Inside The Company: CIA Diary*, London: Penguin, 1975.

Ambler, Eric, *The Levanter,* New York: Atheneum, 1972.

Arathorn, D.W., *Kamal*, New York: Harper and Row, 1972.

Aricha, Amos and Eli Landau, *Phoenix*, New York: Signet, 1979.

Begin, Menachem, *The Revolt*, New York, 1948: 2nd ed. New York: Nash Publishing, Dell, 1977.

Bell, J. Bowyer, *Terror Out of Zion*, New York: Avon Books, 1977.

Bellow, Saul, *To Jerusalem and Back: A Personal Account*, New York: Viking Press, 1976; Penguin, 1977.

Berger, Morroe, *The Arab World Today*, New York: Doubleday, 1962; Anchor, 1964.

Bill, James A., "Iran and the Crisis of 1978," *Foreign Affairs*, Winter 1978/1979.

Black, Lionel, *Arafat is Next!*, New York: Stein and Day, 1975.

Caroz, Yaacov, *The Arab Secret Services*, London: Corgi, Transworld Publishers, 1978.

Charles, Robert, *A Clash of Hawks*, New York: Pinnacle Books, 1975.

Churchill, Randolph S. and Winston S. Churchill, *The Six Day War*, London: Heinemann, 1967.

Clarkson, Geoffrey, *Jihad*, New York: Pinnacle Books, 1981.

Collins, Larry and Dominque Lapierre, *O Jerusalem!* New York: Simon and Schuster, 1972.

Collins, Larry and Dominque Lapierre, *The Fifth Horseman*, New York: Simon and Schuster, 1980.

Copeland, Miles, *The Real Spy World*, London: Sphere, 1974, 1978.

Coppel, Alfred, *The Apocalypse Brigade*, New York: Holt, Rinehart and Winston, 1981, Charter Books, 1983.

Dan, Uri and Edward Radley, *The Eichman Syndrome*, New York: A Leisure Book, 1977.

David, Maggie, *The Sheik*, New York: Fawcett Crest, 1977.

Dayan, Moshe, *Diary of the Sinai Campaign 1965*, New York: Harper & Row, 1966.

Dayan, Moshe, *Moshe Dayan: Story of My Life*, New York: Warner Books, 1977.

Deacon, Richard, *The Israeli Secret Service*, London: Hamilton, 1977.

Eban, Abba, *My Country*, New York: Random House, 1972.

Eisenberg, Dennis, Uri Dan, Eli Landau, *The Mossad: Israel's Secret Intelligence Service*, New York and London: Paddington, 1978.

Eisenberg, Dennis and Menahem Portugali, *Operation Uranium Ship*, London: Corgi, 1978.

Elmessiri, M. Abdelwahab, *The Land of Promise: A Critique of Political Zionism,* New Brunswick, N.J.: North American Press, 1977.

Elmessiri, M. Abdelwahab, ed. *A Lover from Palestine and Other Poems,* Washington, DC: Free Palestine Press, 1970.

Elon, Amos, *Flight into Egypt*, New York: Pinnacle Books, 1981.

Elon, Amos, *Herzl*, New York: Holt, Rinehart and Winston, 1975.

Erdman, Paul, *The Crash of '79*, New York: Pocket Books, 1976.

Fahmy, Ismail, *Negotiations for Peace in the Middle East*, Baltimore: John Hopkins University Press, 1983.

Follett, Ken, *On Wings of Eagles*, New York: Morrow, 1983.

Follett, Ken, *Triple*, New York: Arbor House; Signet, 1980.

Frankel, Sandor and Webster Mews, *The Aleph Solution*, New York: Stein and Day, 1978.

Gehlen, Reinhard, trans. David Irving, *The Service*, New York: Popular Library, 1972.

Goff, Richard, Walter Moss, Janice Terry and Jiu-Hwa Upshur, *The Twentieth Century: A Brief Global History*, New York: Alfred A. Knopf, 1983.

Goldsmith, Barbara, "The Meaning of Celebrity," *The New York Times Magazine*, December 4, 1983.

Greenfield, Richard Pierce and Irving A. Greenfield, *The Life Story of Menachem Begin*, New York: Manor Books, 1977.

Gur, Lt. Gen. Mordechai, *The Battle for Jerusalem*, In Hebrew 1974; New York: Popular Library, 1978.

Haber, Eitan, Zeev Schiff, Ehud Yaari, *The Year of the Dove*, New York: Bantam, 1979.

Haddad, C.A., *The Moroccan*, New York: Harper and Row, 1976; Bantam, 1978.

Hamady, Sania, *Temperament and Character of the Arabs*, New York: Twayne Publishers, 1960.

Harel, Isser, *The House on Garibaldi Street*, New York: Viking and Bantam, 1976.

Harel, Isser, *Jihad*, London: Corgi, 1978.

Harris, Leonard, *The Masada Plan*, New York: Popular Library, 1978.

Hart, Alan, *Arafat: Terrorist or Peacemaker?* London: Sidgwick & Jackson, 1984.

Heikal, Mohamed, *Autumn of Fury: The Assassination of Sadat*, New York: Random House, 1983.

Heikal, Mohamed, *Sphinx and Commissar*, London: Collins, 1978.

Heikal, Mohamed, *The Road to Ramadan*, London: Collins, 1975; New York: Ballantine, 1976.

Irving, Clive, *Promise the Earth*, New York: Ballantine Books, 1982.

Jonas, George, *Vengeance*, New York: Simon and Schuster, 1984.

Kaplan, Howard, *The Damascus Cover*, New York: Fawcett Crest, 1977.

Kiernan, Thomas *Yasir Arafat*, London: ABACUS, Sphere, 1976.

Kloepfer, Marguerite, *The Heart and the Scarab*, New York: Avon, 1981.

Laffin, John, *Rhetoric and Reality: The Arab Mind Considered*, New York: Taplinger Publishing, 1975.

Laffin, John, *The Dagger of Islam*, New York: Sphere, 1979, revised Bantam, 1981.

L'Amour, Louis, *The Walking Drum,* New York: Bantam Books, 1984.

Landau, Jacob M., ed., *Man, State, and Society in the Contemporary Middle East,* New York: Praeger, 1972.

le Carré, John, *The Little Drummer Girl,* New York: Alfred A. Knopf, 1983.

Les Temps Modernes (Special Issue), "Le Conflit Israélo-Arabe," June 1967.

Lev, Igal, *Jordan Patrol* in Hebrew 1970, New York: Modern Literary Editions, 1970.

Lotz, Wolfgang, *The Champagne Spy,* New York: Manor Books, 1973.

Marchetti, Victor and John D. Marks, *The CIA and the Cult of Intelligence,* New York: Dell, 1974.

Markstein, George, *The Goering Testament,* New York: Ballantine, 1981.

McInerny, Ralph, *Lying There,* New York: Charter, 1979.

Michener, James Alberg, *The Source,* New York: Random House, 1965; Fawcett, 1978.

Mitgang, Herbert, "Mergers in the Book World; Still an Unfinished Chapter," *The New York Times,* Sunday, August 19, 1979.

Mortimer, Edward, *Faith and Power: The Politics of Islam,* New York: Vintage, 1982.

Naipaul, V.S., *Among the Believers,* New York: Alfred A. Knopf, 1981; Vintage, 1982.

Nelson, Cynthia, ed., *The Desert and the Sown,* Berkeley: Institute of International Studies, University of California, 1973.

Nijim, Basheer K., "The Jordan Basin and International Riparian Disputes: A Search for Patterns" (Paper delivered at Middle East Studies Association Conference, Columbus, November 1970).

Osmond, Andrew, *Saladin!,* New York: Doubleday, 1976; Bantam, 1979.

Portugali, M. *Khamsin,* London: MacDonald Future, 1981.

Raban, Jonathan, *Arabia Through The Looking Glass,* London: Collins, 1979.

Reynolds, Maxine, *The House in the Kasbah*, New York: Beagle Books, 1972.

Riis, David Allen, *The Jerusalem Conspiracy*, New York: Dell, 1979.

Roberts, Thomas A. *The Heart of the Dog*, New York: Random House, 1972.

Sadat, Anwar el., *In Search of Identity: an Autobiography*, London: Collins, 1978.

Said, Edward, *Covering Islam: How the Media and the Experts Determine How We See the Rest of the World*, New York: Pantheon, 1981.

Schiff, Barry and Hal Fishman, *The Vatican Target*, New York: Fawcett Crest, 1979.

El-Shazly, Lt. Gen. Saad, *The Crossing of the Suez*, San Francisco: American Mideast Research, 1980.

Stein, Benjamin and Herbert Stein, *On The Brink*, New York: Ballantine, 1977.

Steven, Stewart, *The Spymasters of Israel*, New York: Ballantine, 1980.

Stevenson, William, *Strike Zion!* New York: Bantam, 1967.

Stevenson, William, *Zanek!: A Chronicle of the Israeli Air Force*, New York, Bantam, 1971.

Stevenson, William, with Uri Dan, *Ninety Minutes at Entebbe*, New York: Bantam, 1976.

Stewart, Mary, *The Gabriel Hounds*, New York: Mill, 1967; Fawcett Crest, 1968.

Sugar, Andrew, *Israeli Commandos: The Alps Assignment*, New York: Manor Books, 1975.

Suleiman, Michael W., "Fact and Fiction in American Perceptions of the Middle East," (unpublished paper).

Suleiman, Michael W., "Stereotypes, Public Opinion and Foreign Policy," *Action*, February 7, February 14 and February 21, 1983.

Sweet, Louise, ed., *Peoples and Cultures of the Middle East*, 2 vols., New York: The Natural History Press, 1970.

Thompson, Anne Armstrong, *Message From Absalom*, New York: Simon and Schuster, 1975.

Timerman, Jacobo, *The Longest War: Israel in Lebanon*, New York: Alfred A. Knopf, 1982.

Tinan, Edward, "Doubleday Rocks and Rolls," *New York*, February 7, 1983.

Tinnin, David B. with Dag Christensen, *The Hit Team*, New York: Dell, 1976.

Trevanian, *Shibumi*, New York: Ballantine, 1979.

Tuchman, Barbara, "A Task for Arabs," *The New York Times*, July 25, 1982.

Tully, Andrew, *The Super Spies*, New York: Pocket Books, 1970.

Tyrrell, R. Emmett, "Chimera in the Middle East," *Harper's*, November 1976.

Uris, Leon, *Exodus*, New York: Doubleday, 1958; Bantam, 1959.

Uris, Leon, *The Haj*, New York: Doubleday, 1984.

Viertel, Joseph, *The Last Temptation*, New York: Simon and Schuster, 1955; Pocket Books, 1956.

Weizman, Ezer, *On Eagles' Wings*, New York: Berkeley, 1976.

Wolf, Eric Robert, *Peasant Wars of the 20th Century*, New York: Harper and Row, 1969.

Zion, Sidney and Uri Dan, "Israel's Peace Strategy," *The New York Times Sunday Magazine*, April 8, 1979.

Zion, Sidney and Uri Dan, "Untold Story of the Mideast Talks," *The New York Times Sunday Magazine*, January 21 and 28, 1979.

About the Author

Janice J. Terry, Professor of Middle Eastern History at Eastern Michigan University, holds an M.A. in Arab Studies from the American University of Beirut and a Ph.D. from the School of Oriental and African Studies of the University of London. She is the author of *The Wafd, 1919–1952: Cornerstone of Egyptian Political Power,* as well as numerous articles and book chapters on Western media coverage of the Middle East.